The Apostolate of Holy Motherhood

Introduction written and book compiled by:
Mark I. Miravalle, S.T.D.

Published by:
The Riehle Foundation
P.O. Box 7
Milford, OH 45150

NIHIL OBSTAT
Monsignor Joseph P. Malara,
Censor Librorum

IMPRIMATUR
Most Reverend Albert H. Ottenweller, D.D., S.T.L.,
Bishop of Steubenville

June 5, 1991

Published by:
The Riehle Foundation
P.O. Box 7
Milford, Ohio 45150

Library of Congress Catalog Card No.: 91-062526

ISBN: 1-877678-18-X

Table of Contents

MESSAGE NO. PAGE

MESSAGE NO. PAGE

Quote of Mother Teresa of Calcutta on The Apostolate of Holy Motherhood

"From reading portions of the book, I can see how well it is written, so true to the teaching of Mother Church and such an authentic spirituality of what being a mother means in today's world."

Mother Teresa, MC

INTRODUCTION

I. Background

It was after being contacted by the respective authorities that I began a process of preliminary investigation into a series of reported supernatural visions taking place within the continental United States. Visions that if authentic will have a profound and worldwide impact on the nature of one of the most sublime vocations in the human spectrum: the vocation of Christian motherhood.

I received a manuscript of approximately eighty type-written pages which contained messages that were transmitted through a number of reported visions. These visions took place during the months of February through August 1987 (which consisted of the first part of the 1987 Marian Year declared by Pope John Paul II). The manuscript had been sent by the present spiritual director and confessor of the person reporting to have received the visions. The spiritual director requested that a theological study be made into the messages and concurring phenomena to verify that nothing in their contents was in any way contrary to faith and morals as taught by the Magisterium of the Church.

The visions consisted principally of appearances of Jesus Christ and the Blessed Virgin Mary. The initial visions of Jesus were primarily under the appearance of the Christ Child, with the expressed intention of manifesting the tenderness of Jesus' love, as well as fostering a renewed respect for the dignity and value of children in our present tragic age of abortion, child abuse and child neglect of both the physical and spiritual nature. The visionary describes the Christ Child as being very young, somewhere between one and a half and two and a half years of age. He wore a grayish, off-white tunic and sometimes appeared wearing a crown. The visionary described the voice of the Christ Child as being "gentle, but with authority; when He spoke, I immediately did the things He requested because He spoke with such authority."

The Blessed Virgin Mary would normally appear with the Christ Child, holding Him in her arms and would usually reveal a message that would serve to introduce, conclude, or simply compliment the revealed message of the Christ Child. The Blessed Virgin would appear in varied dress, sometimes with a white veil over her head that would wrap across her shoulders, sometimes wearing a crown, or in a traditional image of Our Lady, such as Our Lady of Mt. Carmel or Our Lady of Sorrows.

In the later visions, Our Lord and the Blessed Virgin appear more regularly under the images of the Sacred Heart of Jesus and the Immaculate Heart of Mary. The visionary has remarked that even when Our Lord appeared as a grown man in the image of the Sacred Heart, that His gentleness was greatly manifested: "Even when He was admonishing, it was done with such great gentleness."

The specific visions recorded from February 8, 1987, to August 11, 1987, are the body of messages that are to comprise both this booklet and the proceeding spiritual movement of the "Apostolate of Holy Motherhood in Catholic Families," which we will discuss in greater detail shortly. These principal visions are preceded by a few preliminary visions in the latter part of 1986 and the first part of 1987 which depict Our Lord in His glorified state, Our Lord in His Passion, the Blessed Mother with her Immaculate Heart exposed, as well as visions of various women Saints known for their profound purity: St. Catherine of Siena, St. Anne, and St. Clare of Assisi. Although the visionary has experienced various visions since the period of February to August 1987, she has a certainty that only the messages given during that approximate seven month time period are the specific messages intended by Our Lord and the Blessed Mother to commence the spiritual and silent movement of the "Apostolate of Holy Motherhood in Catholic Families."

II. The Visionary: "Mariamante"

The recipient of the visions and juxtaposed messages which aim at the restoration and sanctification of the vocation of holy motherhood is, most appropriately, a mother. The visionary is a young mother in her middle thirties, with three children whose respective ages, when the visions took place, were seven, three, and one. That the visionary is a young mother bears a significance to the nature of the messages, for at one point when the visionary wondered why so many of her personal questions and difficulties were being answered through these messages, the Blessed Mother responded, "This is because I wish to speak to other mothers through you and your everyday life experiences."

To safeguard the visionary's state in life as a mother of young children, the Blessed Mother assured the visionary that her personal identity would remain confidential. Anyone familiar with the tremendous cross that accompanies the grace of being chosen to receive a private revelation can see the appropriateness of sparing a young mother that public responsibility. This is particularly fitting when the purpose of the revelation is precisely the sanctification of motherhood and the Christian family "from within." For this reason, when referring to this mother-visionary in the text, we will use the title, *"Mariamante,"* which in Latin means "lover of Mary."

During an extensive interview with Mariamante at her home some pertinent information regarding her religious background and upbringing was obtained. She had personally received little to no formal theological or religious education in the Catholic faith. She was born into a Catholic family whose religious practice or fervor was average, limited principally to Sunday Mass attendance. The visionary had not attended Catholic schools during her upbringing, and any religious education was limited to C.C.D. classes. The only adult religious education or formation Mariamante received was during her brief novitiate formation that preceded her entry into the Franciscan Third Order for the laity. Here again, her theological education could not be considered formal nor even begin to reflect the profound level of theological and pastoral insight contained in the revealed messages. It should likewise be noted that since the time of these reported revelations, Mariamante was wisely forbidden by her spiritual director to read any other writings on private revelation, contemporary or otherwise, nor any classical mystical writings in an attempt to protect the integrity and purity of transmission of what was personally taking place in her own spiritual life.

In general, Mariamante seemed very peaceful during our interview, though understandably serious about the nature of the subject matter being discussed. She was interrupted several times by her children, but much like her practice as reflected in the manuscript, she patiently excused herself to tend to the needs of her children and then returned with a focused concentration to our interview in her attempt to give the most accurate and precise answers possible to the ubiquitous and interminable questioning. Externally, Mariamante seems to live an ordinary domestic life as a Christian wife and mother; but it is also a life incarnationally permeated with a charity and humility that is manifest in the way that the many little duties of her life seem to be performed for God, out of love of God. Specific information on Mariamante is contained in the foreword by her spiritual director.

III. The Message: Apostolate of Holy Motherhood in Catholic Families

As the messages began to be conveyed during the visions, the Blessed Virgin instructed Mariamante to "Write this down." Mariamante asked, "Now?" and the Blessed Mother responded, "Yes, now." The messages were recorded verbatim and at one point the Blessed Virgin instructed Mariamante to take the words down in shorthand (a skill she had previously acquired). Hence, the messages are in no way a summary or later paraphrasing of the words of Jesus and Mary, they rather constitute a verbatim recording of the messages as they were being communicated.

The heart of these messages and indeed the overall purpose of the visions is revealed on March 25, 1987, the Feast of the Annunciation. This feast which celebrates the sublime motherhood of the Blessed Virgin Mary in her own maternal gift of human nature to the Word made Flesh, presents the most fitting possible liturgical feast for the revelation of an Apostolate of Holy Motherhood, a spiritual movement anticipated to reach Catholic families in the "four corners of the earth." The following excerpt is taken from the beginning of the March 25th vision of the Christ Child and the Blessed Mother, with this message coming from the Christ Child:

> "It is necessary for you to copy the details of the following discourse accurately for it will serve as the basis for the tenets of the apostolate of motherhood of which we have spoken in the past. It is to be named after My Mother, the Queen of Heaven and Earth, the Mother of God, and will be called the Apostolate of Holy Motherhood in Catholic Families. This Apostolate will be approved by the Holy Father and will be promulgated amongst the families of My Church in the four corners of the earth. It will do great good and help much in stemming the tide of evil ravaging so many families today."

The vision goes on to specify three basic tenets of the Aposto of Holy Motherhood that its members are to follow. These t basic tenets are commented upon as part of an overall summary of the message and movement of Holy Motherhood which was composed by Mariamante under holy obedience at the directive of her spiritual director for his own understanding.[1] The following is the summary text in its original form:

The Heart of the Movement and Major Points of the Apostolate of Holy Motherhood

—An Apostolate of mothers consecrated to the Mother of God for the glory of God
—Pursuit of the Divine Will in their lives
—Contemplative prayer
—Eucharistic Adoration
—Practice of evangelical purity
—Devotion to the Christ Child,
Esteem and appreciation for children
—Devotion to the Holy Family,
Communication of the faith to their children
—Fifteen decade daily Rosary
—Wearing of the Scapular and the Sacred Heart Badge
—Intense sacramental life, frequent Confession and Communion
—Devotion to the Sacred and Immaculate Hearts
—Practice of the Nine First Fridays and Five First Saturdays, reparation for sin
—Devotion to duty
—Fidelity to the Holy Father, the Magisterium, and all the teachings of the Church (both faith and morals)
—Upholding of all the moral teachings of the Church
—Prayers for purity in the world

---

1. During the course of our conversations Mariamante mentioned that it is difficult for her to write anything regarding the visions by way of description or explanation except when directed to do such by her spiritual director in the confessional under holy obedience. Under these conditions the words seem to flow out of her and she is able to recall and record details and contents under a certain degree of inspiration. This summary of the message and heart of the movement of Holy Motherhood was composed under these aforementioned conditions.

—Prayers for the mitigation of suffering of innocent children in the world
—Prayers for priests

An apostolate of mothers called to glorify God and pursue the Divine Will in their lives, who are consecrated to the Mother of God, and practice contemplative prayer and fidelity to duty in an exemplary manner of holiness.

The Heart of the Movement

The three basic tenets of the Apostolate of Holy Motherhood (announced March 25, 1987, during a vision of the Christ Child and Our Blessed Mother):

1. "...they must devote all their time, energy, and resources, including their very selves to the greater glory of God and the pursuit of the Divine Will in their lives;
2. "(they) must be consecrated to My Most Holy Mother under the title of 'Mother of God';
3. "(they) must seek to fulfill their daily duties, that is, as mothers and wives in an exemplary manner of holiness by pursuing the contemplative life in their homes..."

This is a way of perfection for those called to the sublime vocation of motherhood.

God wishes for the exaltation of this vocation to be extolled, motherhood having already been exalted by the second Person of the Blessed Trinity, Jesus Christ's presence in the Holy Family and in the womb of the Blessed Virgin, emphasizing also the great dignity of children. He wishes for this exaltation to be made known, understood, and highly recognized in our day and at this time in history.

God is omnipotent and wishes to transform by His Divine Grace those whom He calls to this movement, the Apostolate of Holy Motherhood, to a higher degree of sanctity through the practice of contemplative prayer in the home, and to transform them into likenesses of His Most Holy Mother by the imitation of her virtues and the gifts of the Holy Spirit and by consecration to her under the title of "Mother of God."

In order to do this He will pour forth His graces on those souls who are so consecrated and receptive and give them His Holy Spirit to a great degree. Extraordinary graces are promised to those members of this Apostolate.

The messages contain all the most necessary aspects of the interior life comprising a virtual catechism of the spiritual life, and a spiritual path which is applicable to the state in life, motherhood, the universal vocation (that vocation from which all people are given life). Particular emphasis to the virtue of purity is given, being referred to by Our Lady as "evangelical purity" which is now necessary. By extolling the virtues of the Blessed Mother and communicating by grace these same virtues to the members of her Apostolate, this movement is meant to play an important role in the Triumph of her Immaculate Heart foretold at Fatima and of God's renewing of the face of the earth.

This is a spiritual movement rather than an organization. The messages will inspire those whom Our Lord and Blessed Mother wish, and aid in opening their hearts for the reception of the extraordinary graces necessary to fulfill this Their divine plan.

One of the major fruits of the movement will be renewed appreciation of and esteem for children and the person of Christ in children, brought about particularly through devotion to the Christ Child. The Holy Family is to be the model for these families. The graces won by the members of this Apostolate will aid in the mitigation of the suffering of innocent children throughout the world, many of whom are now suffering from spiritual neglect as well as those who suffer physical neglect. Children are being impoverished spiritually in the developed world by the materialism and spiritual neglects of their parents. They are not receiving the faith from their parents. This is the most severe neglect, the one which robs the children of eternal life with God in Heaven. God in His Goodness loves in an unfathomable way each one of these precious children and wishes for them to be loved as "precious jewels," which they truly are, by their parents.

In addition to their own families God will apply the graces won by those of this movement to many of those whom He wishes now to reach.

Eucharistic adoration is emphasized as well as frequent reception of the sacraments of Confession and Holy Communion, and a daily fifteen decade Rosary.

Aids in contemplative prayer are given, particularly devotion to the Sacred and Immaculate Hearts and Eucharistic adoration. Of the messages, particularly the Sacred Heart and many of the Christ Child's discourses are well suited to serve as basis for meditation and contemplative prayer.

In order to help usher in the Triumph of the Immaculate Heart of Mary, these mothers and members of this movement will be called upon. Now a movement of mothers in imitation of the Blessed Virgin is necessary to "stem the tide of evil" and to cause holiness to flourish in the world. These mothers will be those called to be cohorts of Our Blessed Mother in the sanctification of the family and the world and in the upbringing of children in holiness.

The devotions to the Nine First Fridays and the Five First Saturdays are given particular emphasis as the means of reparation for sin and the eradication of evil in the world today. Also a fifteen decade daily Rosary and the use of sacramentals, the Scapular and the Sacred Heart badge are stressed.

The truths expounded upon in these messages and the guidance given to the interior life are in complete conformity to the teachings of the Holy Catholic Church. Much of the information given is applicable to all persons who are serious about the interior life, the way of perfection, and a life of holiness, and is not limited to mothers alone. Indeed, some of the messages are even directed to priests in general, and prayers for priests are also requested.

In this way, by the pursuit of the Divine Will in their lives and the practice of virtue, coupled with an intense prayer life and adherence to daily duty, the sanctification of the individual, the family, and in turn the world will be aided.

So may the hearts of these mothers, called to this silent apostolic work, be as gardens for Our Lord where He can come and repose, even as He reposed His Sacred Head near the Heart of His Mother Mary while on earth.

Praised be Jesus Christ now and forever. Amen.

In this summary of the message and movement by Mariamante, we note firstly that the Apostolate that is to come as a result of these messages is not to be organizational, but rather a spiritual movement, a silent movement of domestic sanctification that takes place through the humble and dedicated living of the message by mothers. Again, the cornerstone of living the message of Holy Motherhood is found in the three basic tenets as listed by Mariamante. In regards to the fulfillment of the second basic tenet, "they must be consecrated to My Most Holy Mother under the title, 'Mother of God,' " Mariamante received under inspiration (something short of inner locution but more than any ordinary movement of the soul), a prayer of Consecration to the Mother of God that appears in this booklet immediately following the text of the messages. Although this may be considered a preferred prayer of consecration, as it appears to be particularly given for this Apostolate, nonetheless, any legitimate form of Marian consecration with the insertion of the title, "Mother of God" would appear to fulfill this second basic tenet.

The theological nature of the message represents both an unambiguous orthodoxy and complete obedience to the Pope and the official teaching authority of the Church, the Magisterium. In the June 24, 1987 message, the Blessed Mother refers to the Holy Father as the "crowning glory of my movement, the Pope I love so dearly, and the one to whom you must refer for all guidance in matters of faith and morals. Give him your unswerving loyalty as my Son's true representative on earth, which he is." The theological soundness of the message has been confirmed by a number of recognized orthodox Catholic theologians (the statements of whom appear in the early pages of this booklet), as well as by the *Nihil Obstat* and the *Imprimatur* which this booklet has received, as was specifically requested in the body of messages.

In the final analysis, all the principal criteria for an authentic private revelation seem to be strongly present in the Apostolate of Holy Motherhood in Catholic Families. At this point in the introduction of the Apostolate, our own question may be similar to that of Mariamante's as these supernatural events began taking place in her life: "How do I know this is from you, Mother?" The response of the Blessed Mother, at once so simple and so sublime like so much of this message and Apostolate, returns us to the first and ultimate criteria for an authentic private revelation, the truth of the message: "You will know this is from me by the truth in it."

Let us commend this work to St. Joseph, Patron of all Christian families, and designated in the text as a special patron of the Apostolate. May the Apostolate of Holy Motherhood imitate the way of St. Joseph, who in silence and obscurity, in humility and perseverance, did all for the glory of God and the salvation of souls in his sanctified pursuit and attainment of the goal of Christian life: the perfection of love in Christian Holiness.

Mark Miravalle, S.T.D.
Associate Professor of Theology and Mariology
Franciscan University of Steubenville

FOREWORD

What is more glorious than a Mother? The late, saintly Joseph Cardinal Mindszenty described her as "The most important person on earth. She cannot claim the honor of having built Notre Dame Cathedral. She need not. She has built something more magnificent than any Cathedral—a dwelling for an immortal soul, the tiny perfection of her baby's body."

The Angels have not been blessed with such a grace. They cannot share in God's creative miracle to bring new saints to Heaven. Only a human mother can. Mothers are closer to God than any other creature. God joins forces with mothers in perfecting this act of creation.

What on God's good earth is more glorious than this: to be a mother?

A newspaper reporter went to interview the mother of the saintly author of this beautiful tribute to a mother after he had been condemned to life imprisonment. "I ask myself so many times," the aged woman told him, "how the good Lord could ever have turned to the home of poor farmers such as we are, and there found a priest with the Church as the sole object and preoccupation of his entire priestly and episcopal life."

When asked if she knew where her son was then located, she remained silent. Then pointing to the Sacred Heart, she said: "He knows where the Cardinal is. Others know it too—those for whom I pray to the Lord every day. I must keep quiet; I talk only to the Lord Who knows everything."

This woman was a heroine. I am sure that there are many other mothers who attain such sublime heights in their maternal vocation. For too long, holiness has been considered a monopoly of the religious life and of the priesthood. Numerous conciliar Fathers of Vatican II reacted against this discretionary concept. It is the whole Church, every member of the Mystical Body of Christ who should be holy. The Sermon on the Mount is a charter of perfection for everyone, without exception. The Church of today needs saints everywhere. The laity in particular is called to witness before the whole world to an outstanding holiness. Marriage is a holy state ordained of God. It makes husband and wife co-partners with God in bringing His future sons and daughters into the world. What a glorious concept! No greater honor could be given. With this honor comes the tremendous responsibilities of loving and caring for those children so that they may learn their duty as citizens and what they must do to return to their Heavenly Father. They must be taught to understand the Gospel of Jesus Christ and to accept and live His teachings.

It is of great concern to all to save the Christian home at a time when Satan is using every nefarious and insidious propaganda to lure women away from their responsibilities and belittles the role of Motherhood, all of which is the devil's way of destroying woman, the home (a domestic church), and the family—the basic unit of society.

This book contains the messages of Our Lord and His Most Holy Mother to Mariamante, a chosen soul, whom Heaven has selected to further the Apostolate of Holy Motherhood. She is a simple woman, a wife, a mother and housewife. She accepted her mission with humility and obedience to the priests who directed her soul. Divine Providence led her in a miraculous way to her present spiritual director. In the last several years did he become aware that the charisma of his spiritual daughter is genuine. Efforts were made to consult theologians in regard to the genuineness of these messages communicated to her from Heaven. The manuscripts were submitted to a number of them who responded favorably.

In the Apostolate of Holy Motherhood, mothers are called upon not only to be Marthas, but like Mary to practice contemplative prayer and fidelity to their duties in an exemplary manner of holiness. Consecrated to Mary, the Mother of God, they are asked to follow Her as their model for the sanctification of marriage and family life. These mothers will hopefully become members of "the legion of little souls, victims of merciful Love, who will become as numerous as the stars of Heaven and sands of the seashore. It will be terrible to Satan; it will help the Blessed Virgin to crush his head completely" (St. Therese, the Little Flower).

These messages are intended to lead, not only Mothers, but also all other Christians, including the leaders of the Church, to a more fervent observance of the laws of God and a more perfect imitation of the Person of Christ and His Blessed Mother Mary.

May Mary, the Mother of God, "intercede before Her Son in the fellowship of all the Saints, until all families of people, whether they are honored with the title of Christian or whether they still do not know the Saviour, may be happily gathered together in peace and harmony into one People of God, for the glory of the most Holy and Undivided Trinity" (Lumen Gentium, 69).

F.S.D.

Statements on the Messages of the Apostolate of Holy Motherhood by Recognized Catholic Theologians

"I could not possibly object to any doctinal position and I have found no fault in this formulation, on the contrary, everything seems to me to point towards a very orthodox and much needed form of Christian spirituality."

Rev. Michael O'Carroll, C.S.Sp.
Internationally Recognized Mariologist,
Member of the International Mariological Society

"The practical wisdom given in the revelations of the Apostolate of Holy Motherhood show how to respond to the secularized environment dominated by the search for recreation, useless talking, TV values, group therapy for every problem—by turning to the Lord in prayer, especially the Rosary, and repentance, by Eucharistic adoration and the Sacrament of Confession, by devotion to the Hearts of Jesus and Mary, obedience to the Church's teaching and authority and faithfulness to our daily duties."

Rev. George Kosicki, C.S.B.
Apostles of Divine Mercy

"The work contains no doctrinal error against faith and morals as taught by the Magisterium and has received the Imprimatur in this regard. The work manifests a profound Catholic spirituality of motherhood and of the overall life of the Domestic Church."

Dr. Mark I. Miravalle, S.T.D.
Professor of Theology and Mariology
Franciscan University of Steubenville

"Always obedient to the judgement of the Church, in these messages I find Mary's call to Christian motherhood refreshing and inspiring."

Rev. Giles Dimock, O.P.
Professor of Theology at the Angelicum, Rome
and Holy Apostles Seminary

"Though I in no way wish to anticipate the judgement of the Church on the supernatural origin of these messages, there is no doubt that their strong call to holiness of family life and Christian motherhood echoes the purest Gospel message and is desperately needed in today's world."

Rev. George T. Montague, S.M.
Professor of Theology and Scripture
St. Mary's University, San Antonio, Texas

Preliminary Visions to the Revelation of the Apostolate of Holy Motherhood[1]

1. Our Lord as an adult. His face was most beautiful and He was dressed in flowing robes. I saw Him at ______ Catholic Church when praying in front of the statue of Our Blessed Mother. I had this vision at least twice in December of 1986. I had great peace and joy afterwards.

2. Our Lord in death on the Cross with His head hanging straight down. This was most sorrowful. I believe this was also in December of 1986. This took place also at ______ Catholic Church while praying in front of the Blessed Sacrament.

3. Our Lord's face in death, His features resembling in appearance those of the Shroud of Turin. This vision was only of His Sacred Face. It took place at home while I was praying in front of the Pilgrim Virgin of Fatima statue. This, I think, had something to do with Father having told me not to make a thanksgiving after Mass in the church, due to the state I was going into (which I now understand was ecstasy). This, of course, he had to do because people were becoming alarmed, thinking I had fainted, although it was from having gone to Holy Communion that this was happening to me. This vision also took place in December of 1986.

4. Several visions of the Blessed Mother with her Immaculate Heart exposed. These were in January of 1987. During one of these visions, I understood that I should ask Father to consecrate the fraternity to the Immaculate Heart of Mary. These took place at home while praying in front of the same Virgin of Fatima statue.

---

1. These visions were recorded on February 18, 1987 although they took place before that date.—Mariamante.

5. I also had several visions of different women who were dressed in various garb. After having these I felt I should pray to certain Saints. Sometimes I know immediately who the Saints are that I am seeing, and sometimes I don't know but eventually find out after repetitive visions. The following ones took place at home and were in January and the first week of February, 1987. They were as follows:

   a. St. Catherine of Siena, dressed in medieval garb, with a veil and a white cloth that surrounded her face.

   b. St. Clare of Assisi, in a habit, also with a cloth around her face and swathing material at her throat. She had a most noble appearance and when I saw her I said, "She must be an abbess."

   c. An older woman who I saw repeatedly and was dressed like the Blessed Mother. I think she may have been St. Anne, because afterwards I felt strongly that I should pray to her that week, even going so far as to consecrate my family to her and to say her litany. This I had never done before, never having had a particular devotion to her before these visions occurred.

   d. I also saw myself in a vision dressed in ancient garb similar to the Blessed Mother's. I somehow understood this to mean that I was being fashioned into the likeness of the Blessed Mother.[2] This occurred several times.

The four visions above occurred in sets of several at a time, one following the other.

---

2. Later, I understood that all mothers, and particularly those called to this Apostolate, are meant to become living images of Our Blessed Mother through the power of the Holy Spirit and by the imitation of Our Blessed Mother's virtues.—Mariamante.

1

Sunday
February 8, 1987

"Evangelical Purity"

Vision of Our Blessed Mother with the following message and dialogue:[3]

Blessed Mother: "*Evangelical purity* is to be practiced especially among women and priests, and all who are called to be spouses of Christ."[4]

Mariamante: "How do I know this is from you, Mother?"

Blessed Mother: "You will know by the truth in it."

Mariamante: "Should I tell Father[5] about this, and what will his reaction be?"

Blessed Mother: "Yes, at first it may be difficult, but in the end he will understand. There must be purity among relationships and the way persons relate to one another. It is not necessary to discuss the impurity of today's society in depth or publicly."

Mariamante: At this point, I said something to the effect of worrying about pride. Her answer was:

Blessed Mother: "Do not worry about it. It is being taken care of."

Mariamante: I then expressed some concern about me being picked to deliver a message about purity and said: "Mother, you were pure from the moment of conception." Her answer was:

Blessed Mother: "Yes, this is true, but you are being made pure by the graces in the confessional."

Mariamante: "But I am not worthy to be picked to do this."

---

3. I had to go back and write this from memory after the vision ended.—Mariamante.

4. I later thought that there was some significance in having seen the three women Saints the previous week as models of this purity she spoke of. They also represented women in all states of life: St. Catherine of Siena as a single laywoman; St. Clare of Assisi as a nun; and St. Anne as a married woman. (See Preliminary Visions [#5] for description of aforementioned vision.)—Mariamante.

5. The priest who is Mariamante's spiritual director. When the term "Father" is used in relation to Mariamante, it is always referring to the priest who is her spiritual director.—Ed.

Blessed Mother: "Yes, this is also true, but you are being made worthy by Jesus."

Mariamante: "Will you help me to remember all of this?"

Blessed Mother: "Yes, I will; but begin to write this down as soon as you can."

2

Tuesday
February 10, 1987

"His Sacred Face"

Vision of Our Lord at ______ Catholic Church similar to the ones in December, although His Sacred Face seemed more solemn and not quite as youthful, although this may have been due to the expression on His Face.

3

Wednesday, February 11, 1987
Feast of Our Lady of Lourdes

"Pray For And Practice Purity"

Visions of Our Blessed Mother and two other women, who I felt were St. Bernadette and St. Anne, with the following dialogue:

Blessed Mother: "Pray for and practice purity. The world depends upon it now. Pray to the Saints who were models and examples of purity. They will help you and so will I."

Mariamante: "How do I know this is from you and I am not being deceived?"

Blessed Mother: "I come from Him Who can neither deceive nor be deceived. It is important to tell Father everything that transpires now. Do not be afraid. Rest in my Immaculate Heart and I shall protect you. You will know this is from me by the truth in it. It is for the purpose of humility that the visions are not always clear. You will know in time who they are. It must be this way for now. That is all for now. Be a model mother. It is important to be a good mother."

4

Thursday
February 12, 1987

"Pray For The World"

Vision of Our Blessed Mother:

Blessed Mother: "Pray for the world not just for yourselves."

5

Friday
February 13, 1987

"Say A Fifteen Decade Rosary Daily"

Vision of Our Blessed Mother:

Blessed Mother: "Do not neglect my Son's Passion. Meditate upon it always. Unite yourselves to His Passion. This is your means of salvation."

Mariamante: "Mother, are you angry with me[6]?"

Blessed Mother: "No, but you must be receptive, rather than questioning. Write this down."

Mariamante: "Now?"

Blessed Mother: "Yes, now. My Son suffered horribly for your sins. You must make atonement for them. Do not neglect your duties. They are most important. *Say a fifteen decade Rosary daily.* This is most pleasing to God. Write this legibly. It is important. Tell Father everything.

"Heaven is most distressed with the state the world is in. It is very bad right now. Only prayer and penance can change this. Be attentive to your children. They are most important. They will live during the Reign of my Immaculate Heart. This is a prelude to the ushering in of the Reign of the Sacred Heart. Tell this to Father. I want him to notify others soon, but not now. I will let him know when. Write in shorthand if necessary. Do not be afraid. You have nothing to fear. I love you and will protect you always from the public eye. Father may not fare so well in this regard. He may have to suffer in this regard among his peers. This is due to the state of the world and the

---

6. I thought she might be angry with me for having asked so many questions the other day.—Mariamante.

Church right now. There are other holy priests being called upon to do the same. This is the way it must be. They are most like my Son. I love them dearly and will enfold them in my Immaculate Heart for eternity."

"That is all for now. Tend to your child. Heaven is pleased with holy families."

My baby interrupted at the end right before she said, "That is all. . ." Shortly afterward as I was sitting on the couch, I heard the words, "Write down only what occurs during the visions," although the vision had ended.

6

Saturday
February 14, 1987

"The Eucharist Must Be Adored"

Vision of Our Blessed Mother looking very sad, with many folds in her veil around her face (reminding me of the famous Pieta). She appeared to have been crying:

Blessed Mother: "Tomorrow I am leaving you in this wonderful image, the image of Our Lady of Fatima; but do not fear, I shall be with you. The message of Fatima is most important for this time.

"Humility is a wonderful virtue. Practice humility. Pray for the world. It is urgent now. The world is facing a grave cataclysm beyond known proportion due to the impiety and impurity. I have come to rescue the world from this fate. God has given me this mission. You are my sons and daughters. I do not want to see you perish. The message of Fatima contains all that is necessary for you to know in this time.

"*The Eucharist must be adored. Adore the Eucharist. The Eucharistic Heart of Jesus is the greatest gift God has given to men.* Sadly, it is now not appreciated. This is a grave tragedy. My Son shed His blood for your sins. The least you can do is adore His Eucharistic Heart in the tabernacle.

"The churches are locked. This is another tragedy. People should be praying in front of the tabernacle day and night for the salvation of the world, and especially for purity in the West."

At this point, my baby interrupted.

Blessed Mother: "In the future only do this[7] when the baby is sleeping. Your duty comes first. That is all for now. Finish your Rosary."

7 *Sunday, February 15, 1987*
Approximately 10:30 A.M.

"Humility And Purity Are What Is Needed"

Vision of Sorrowful Mother dressed much like the statue of the Pieta at _____ Catholic Church. She had a grief-stricken expression on her face towards the end of the vision:

Blessed Mother: "I wish to continue my teaching on humility. *Humility and purity are what is needed now in the world. Without them there can be no true love. Say many Rosaries for this purpose.* I will give you great humility personally, so that it will be clear that this message is from me and not from you. Tell Father not to worry. He needs to trust in me alone. I will take care of everything."

Mariamante: I expressed some hesitancy at telling him this, not wanting to tell him what to do, although I cannot now remember the words. Her answer was this:

Blessed Mother: "Tell him this is from his Mother who loves him dearly and wishes to protect him in all circumstances, but due to the world situation, he must suffer somewhat. I want this message to be spread. I will tell him how later. It is tailored for your time and will be helpful to many in fulfilling my Son's requests. Do not fear. You will be given a certainty and the visions will continue.

"Love your neighbor. Charity must prevail. There is no time for pettiness. Be forgiving towards one another. I am preparing many souls to do great things for God. To Him alone be glory and honor and praise now and forever.

"You will be scrutinized, but do not fear. I will hand-pick the priests to be involved with this my project of both sorrow and love. Be humble towards your Father. Do not give him advice. Let me speak to him through the visions. He has been given charge over your soul. This is no small task. But I will give him joy. I will continue to renew the gift I gave him at Fatima.

7. Meaning writing down the messages.—Mariamante.

He is one of my favorite sons picked long ago, which is why I called him to Fatima.

"Be obedient to your husband also as long as it is not contrary to faith or morals. He is having some difficulty now, but will soon begin to understand the true faith. Even as I was obedient to St. Joseph while on earth, as when we fled into Egypt. All authority comes from God. This is important for your time.

"My heart is overcome with grief over the state of the world. Pray with me for your salvation. Behold the Eucharistic Heart of Jesus which has loved men so much and adore Him. Go now and prepare for Mass."

8

Later same day
Sunday, February 15, 1987 5:00 P.M.

"Silence And Obscurity"

Vision of Our Blessed Mother, she again appeared to have been crying as the day before:

Blessed Mother: "Silence and obscurity. This is what I ask of you. Let the light of the Lord shine through you in your daily duties. Many misunderstand this and think that they must be in the public eye to do great things for God. It is often quite the contrary. Silence and obscurity—as I was in Bethlehem and Nazareth.

"So many of my priest sons wish to leave their mark in the world rather than preaching the Gospel of my Son. This is an error. My Son has revealed everything. There is nothing new. They should be following in His footsteps rather than forging their own path. They are leading many astray through their errors. Tell them Jesus is the light, not the human mind. They worship the human intellect rather than God Himself.

"Mothers, teach your children to be kind to one another. The important lessons are learned at home. Do not expect others to teach your children. This is your responsibility and should be your joy. The world has taken the joy out of parenting. This is an error. Discipline is necessary, but so is joy. Love your children. Many children are suffering from lack of love. This is a tragedy. They are made to feel as burdens. Their parents should beg God for forgiveness, for he who leads the little ones astray will be held to account for it. Love and cherish your children.

They are great gifts from God. Follow the example of the Holy Family who lived in humility and love, deferring to one another.

"Continue to pray for the world. I love this Holy Father very much. Follow his example. It is everyone's responsibility to be holy.

"Go now and be with your children. They need you."[8]

9

Monday, February 16, 1987
Vision ended at 5:33 P.M.

"Behold My Mother!"

Vision of the Christ Child in His Mother's arms:

Christ Child: "Behold My Mother! I have given her this power and mission to intercede for the world. She acts on your behalf. She acts as the Spouse of the Holy Spirit beckoning My return.

"It is true that I alone have saved the world, but she continually intercedes for you before the throne of God.

"Listen to what she has told you at Fatima and other major apparitions. These will help you to follow My Gospel. Her intercession is a blessing to the world. Only God could conceive of such mercy, to give you such a tender Mother to intercede on your behalf. She makes recompense for your sins by her intercessions; but it is true that you must still atone for them. My Father is too offended. This cannot go on.

"Go to Confession. You need to cleanse your souls of sin. This is the merciful means I have given you to do so. Pray for purity. Impurity offends My Mother and I can tolerate no more. Pray for the sake of your children.

"My Mother is the Queen of Heaven and Earth. Listen to her and put her words into action. This can change everything. Follow the Gospel life that I lived while on earth.

"I will bless the world again as I did at Fatima. Each will have a chance to repent. You are living in an era of extraordinary mercy. Make good use of it and repent. Listen to My Mother and your Mother. She will help you to love Me as you should."

---

8. Towards the end of the vision when she was talking about mothers, I saw myself also, dressed in ancient garb similar to the Blessed Mother's as I have described before.—Mariamante.

Tuesday, February 17, 1987
Approximately 12 Noon

10

Silent Vision

A brief silent vision of Our Lord at ______ Catholic Church. As on February 10, He appeared solemn.

Thursday, February 19, 1987
3:00-4:45 P.M.

11

"The Scapular And The Rosary"

Vision of Our Blessed Mother wearing a crown and dressed in white flowing robes, seen while praying before a statue of Our Lady of Mt. Carmel:

Blessed Mother: "You are not alone. Many are being called upon to do the same."

Mariamante: "Mother, I am not prepared."[9]

Blessed Mother: "From now on be prepared before you begin your Rosary. Write down the dialogue including your words. This is important. I wish to show the tenderness of my love for my children. You will not always remember what you write. This is all right. Do not fear. It is from me.

"I do not wish to interrupt your Rosary during the *Our Fathers* because I want to say it with you. I am the Queen of Heaven and Earth, but I too must obey God. If I obey God, why do not my children on earth do the same? It is so simple. God asks so little of you. He is your merciful Father. Go to Him in all your needs. He wishes to help you, never to harm. It is only because of divine justice that things are the way they are in the world. This is not God's making. It is your own. Sin causes the misery, not God.

"Do not worry, my children who are living the proper life. You will be spared. *The Scapular of Mt. Carmel is a sign of my protection.* Wear it always. It will help you to do good because it is a sign of my love and will remind you of me often. This is the purpose of all sacramentals—to remind you of the person

9. Meaning that I had no pen or paper to write on.—Mariamante.

behind them and to help you to imitate their virtues. The Scapular and the Rosary are the greatest of these and will afford you the most protection. I want all my children to wear one. It will help them to love Jesus more. This is a simple means by which God helps His children. Wear it always. That is all for now. Finish your Rosary."

Mariamante: "Help my faith, Mother."

Blessed Mother: "I will."

12

Friday, February 20, 1987
Approximately 3:30 P.M.

"The Christ Child's Face...Coming To Life"

Vision of the Christ Child. While praying before the same statue of Our Lady of Mt. Carmel as the previous day, the Christ Child's face suddenly changed, coming to life,[10] and I received the following message:

Christ Child: "My Passion was the culmination of..."

This was interrupted when my son got hurt and I had to go to him.

10. The Christ Child's face coming to life was similar to that which occurred on February 16.—Mariamante.

13

Same day
Friday, February 20, 1987 9:20-10:20 P.M.

"Rest In My Immaculate Heart"

Vision of the Blessed Mother with the Christ Child in Her arms with the following message:

Blessed Mother: "Do not worry about being scrutinized. You are my child and I love you and will protect you. I love all my children. My Son, the tenderest of all children, beckons you to listen to me. My Heart is overcome with grief. Please help me to save you as my Son instructed. He holds the keys to the Kingdom of Heaven[11] in His little hands. He has passed them to the Catholic Church. Listen to your priests. They are here to guide you. My Son's Passion was the culmination of the age of which He spoke while on earth. This is the new age of which He spoke, the Reign of my Immaculate Heart and His Sacred Heart."

Mariamante: "My Mother, please help me, I am having difficulty tonight."

Blessed Mother: "I know that you are. Just relax and rest in my Immaculate Heart. There is nothing to fear. It is I. You are far from the state in which you could fare this all in the natural sense, hence, the reason for the way we are communicating. My Heart shall be your refuge and lead you deep into the recesses of the Sacred Heart of my Beloved Son...

"You need not fear the deceit of the enemy as long as you remain in holy obedience. This is indeed your protection. Never forget this. This is an aspect of Church life which is falling by the wayside, yet it is very important for your protection and as a mortification of the will. Obedience is the virtue by which the Saints were mortified. This is a foreign concept to the modern world. How unfortunate this is. Indeed, my Son was obedient even unto death on the Cross, and you are disobedient in the littlest of ways. Learn this virtue well. It will bring you very close to God, which should be the aim of all persons, not just a few. Practice humility and obedience and you will rise speedily to perfection. This should be the aim of all my priest

---

11. The Christ Child appeared to be holding something in His hand. —Mariamante.

sons whom I love so dearly. They are so special to me. That is all on obedience for now. Practice it well and you need not fear anything.

"Today is a day of suffering and atonement. Try to atone for some of the sin in the world always, but particularly on Fridays."[12]

14

Saturday, February 21, 1987
10:30 A.M.

"Pray To Me As The Christ Child"

Vision of the Christ Child in His Mother's arms:

Christ Child: "You need not fear. It is My Mother who speaks to you. She wishes to establish a greater rapport with her children in order to usher in the Triumph. This is necessary due to the wickedness which exists today. Indeed it is her direct intervention into the affairs of men which is now necessary to combat this. She will help you in all your necessities. Go to her. I need not explain this fully. This has always been the teaching of the Church. Go to her now and always. She will help you. Be not afraid to call upon her in all circumstances. Her intercession is most powerful."

At this point, I had started to say my Rosary again because there was a pause in the dialogue, when He said:

Christ Child: "You need not say your Rosary while I am speaking to you. Just listen and I will speak to you.

"She will help you to do God's will. You must all do God's will now if you wish to avert disaster. How sad it is to see so many of you in sin. It grieves My Heart! Please repent before it is too late. I want you all to be spared. I love you. Never forget that I died on the Cross for you out of love. This type of love the world finds hard to understand, yet it is the most real. Indeed, it is the only true love, as all love proceeds from God in His Goodness.

"I bless you all from My Heart. *Devotion to Me as a Child is important for it manifests the tenderness of My love. Pray to Me as the Christ Child. This is most pleasing to Me. Cultivate this devotion."*

---

12. There was also a private conversation which was not fully recorded. —Mariamante.

15

Sunday, February 22, 1987
10:30 A.M.

"Triumph Of My Immaculate Heart"

Vision of Our Blessed Mother wearing a crown:

Blessed Mother: "Your Father did right to prevent this from happening to you in public.[13] The wickedness of men would destroy my plan if possible but my power given to me by God Himself is infinitely greater than all the wickedness in the world. Good always triumphs over evil. Remember this always. It will give you great heart to know and reflect upon this. Satan and his legions cannot prevent my Triumph as hard as they may try, because God Himself has preordained that this should occur in this time. You are fortunate to be living in this time, this era of mercy and love. Not all have been given so great a chance to repent from so much evil.

"You will know by the sign in the heavens which is I myself that the time is at hand for the instantaneous conversion of the multitude. This I will accomplish through a tremendous outpouring of grace upon the earth given at the hands of God to me for this purpose. This will be the Triumph of my Immaculate Heart of which I spoke at Fatima.

"You must do all that I tell you now. It is very important that you follow my instructions, as this will be an aid to many in softening their hearts in order to be receptive to such grace."

Mariamante: "O, Mother, this is so important, please make sure I record it according to God's will and your holy plan."

Blessed Mother: "I will."

Mariamante: "Mother, can this all be possible?"

Blessed Mother: "All things are possible with God, and at my intercession.

"This is part of my plan so do not be concerned about it being fulfilled. I will see to it myself. These are all my special sons and holy priests indeed who are working for my Triumph and being instrumental in saving many souls. They will respond positively and quickly to my plan as they have in the past.

---

13. Meaning ecstasy after reception of Holy Communion—Father had told me to ask God to not let this happen to me in public—as I was thinking about this when I began my Rosary.—Mariamante.

"______[14] will give Father the money to go to Rome, as I wish her to be instrumental in this, as she has been a tireless worker for my cause for so long. See the mercy of your Mother, how she wishes to reward you in even the smallest tasks if they are carried out in love for me and my Son. To Him be all glory and honor and praise now and forever. He has saved you from your sins. Worship Him in love now and in eternity. So be it. Go and contact Father today."

16

Later same day
Sunday, February 22, 1987 4:45 P.M.

"I Bless This Most Holy Church Founded By My Son"

Blessed Mother: "I am speaking directly to your soul. This is by no ordinary means. Although God has given me this power, I have seldom used it in the past—as it was not necessary in a more pious age when the Church was revered. Sadly, this is now not the case. This is why I must employ other means to speak to my children."

At this point, there was an interruption by family members who had just come in, so I said:

Mariamante: "Mother, will you continue later?"

Blessed Mother: "Yes, I will."

Later she continued when I was alone:

Blessed Mother: "God has given me the power to touch the hardest of hearts. Indeed, it has always been this way down through the ages. However, it is ever so urgent now, that I must employ extraordinary means by which to reach my children so hardened in sin.

"I am speaking to many souls now throughout the world to accomplish my plan of salvation of this generation. I say salvation, yes, because without my intercession now, many would be lost for eternity. God in His mercy has preordained this plan to be accomplished by me and, therefore, it is by divine inspiration that I act—always in accord with the will of God, as

14. The Blessed Mother referred to this person by her first name.—Mariamante.

I was from the moment of my being brought into existence by His almighty power.

"*The Holy Father* has declared this a Marian Year. This is at the inspiration of the Holy Spirit which he acts. He *is the sovereign leader of the Church.* He has been given this authority by God Himself. Follow his inspiration. *He will lead you to an ever greater love of me and my Divine Son.* I bless this most Holy Church founded by my Son while He was on earth, from my Heart. O, how I wish that I could persuade all my priest sons to return to their Rosaries. But so many have become hardened in sin, it grieves me. They have forgotten how to pray. I plead with them from a mother's heart to return to prayer. This alone will save them. See my tears.[15] I cry for their souls once so spotless and pure and now defiled by sin. Purity and humility, obedience and poverty, prayer and penance—this will lead them back to my Son Who also loves them so.

"I exhort you all, all my faithful followers, pray for my priests that they all return to me, and I will lead them to Jesus. Behold the mercy of God. He wishes to save you from destruction at the hands of His Mother. I pray for you all from my Heart.

"The Rosary is most powerful now. Use it as your weapon to combat all evil."

Mariamante: "Mother, I love you."

Blessed Mother: "And I love you. Offer this Rosary for all priests throughout the world. Pray for them often in your daily prayers, and I will pray with you for them, so beloved and dear are they to me."

15. Streams of tears ran from the corners of her eyes at this point in the vision.—Mariamante.

17

Monday, February 23, 1987
10:40-11:30 A.M.

"Pray For The Protection Of Innocent Children"

Vision of the Christ Child, wearing a crown, in His Mother's arms:

Christ Child: "I am the Christ Child. See the joy which proceeds from Me. I wish you to be joyous even in your trials and tribulations. This may seem difficult to understand, but if you unite your suffering to Mine, I will turn it into joy. This is part of the mystery of suffering which the world cannot understand. Christian suffering has meaning and is redemptive. In fact, it is necessary for your salvation, for he who would follow Me must take up his cross. Love is stern as death as the Scriptures tell you.

"Love knows no bounds and embraces suffering when it comes, knowing its value. You are wise not to ask of it though, as it may not be God's will. Never seek what may not be God's will. Pray always that God's will be done and accomplished in you. However, you must embrace it when it comes your way. My Father's plan is unique for each one of you. No two are the same. This is another mystery, the mystery of God's creative power.

"I wish to establish in the world greater devotion to Me as the Christ Child. This will be helpful in combating the evils perpetrated against innocent children which are so sadly common now. The innocence of children must be guarded as a precious jewel, for, indeed, it is of infinite more value. Pray for the protection of innocent children who suffer now, even at the hands of those who should love them. They are most like Me in their innocent suffering. Their suffering must be mitigated as divine justice dictates. Help them with your prayers and with action when God puts them in your path.

"This will happen frequently from now on. I will tell you how I wish you to aid them when the time comes. Do not fear. This is part of My plan of rescuing little ones from the jaws of evil. They are most like Me. I will tell you how to help them. This will be a great joy to you, an apostolate of its own. But as all divine plans for earth require human hands, I have chosen you to implement this one. I will tell you more later. You will be instrumental but many will be involved. Help Me to mitigate the sufferings of the innocent, and I will repay you in full. *At the end of each Rosary say three Hail Marys for the mitiga-*

tion of the suffering of the innocent children in the world—so precious and dear are they to My Mother and I. Often throughout your daily duty, say, 'This is for the innocent children suffering in the world.'

"Although I am your Redeemer, I too pray to your Heavenly Father for them as they are most like Me in My childhood when lived on earth. Your salvation is being continuously worked out through the power of prayer and good works. You must not neglect this aspect of the Christian life. They must be accomplished together.

"My Mother has instructed you of many things. Continue to listen to everything she tells you, and she will bring you ever closer to Me and your heavenly reward. I bless you from My Heart. That is all for now. Go in peace."[16]

18

Almost immediately after He finished
Monday, February 23, 1987 11:35-11:45 A.M.

"Greater Devotion To My Immaculate Heart"

Vision of Our Blessed Mother:

Blessed Mother: "My Son wishes to establish greater devotion to my Immaculate Heart. Listen carefully to my instructions as they unfold before you. There will be times when it will be necessary to do things speedily. Tell this to Father. He must act when I tell him so as not to waste any time. This may be difficult for him to understand but it is of great importance. I want him to tell ______ of this and that I wish for him to publish this booklet and begin distribution as soon as possible. There may be some delays in obtaining the Imprimatur but it will be granted. This is why I wish to act quickly.

"You must be prepared. You will be receiving many messages now, sometimes several times per day. I will arrange for the time when your children and husband do not need your attention. Your Mother can do all things with the grace of God.

---

16. There was also a brief personal conversation of which my spiritual director was informed, but which I prefer not to write because it pertains to family members. During this time He also said, "Never be scrupulous in your writing of this message, as I will ensure that what you write is from Me."—Mariamante.

"This is very important as I wish to have as many of my children as possible begin to read this message. It will help them to become holier and to aid in my Triumph. Do not worry about the Imprimatur, I will arrange for it and it will be granted. That is all for now. Tell Father all of this as soon as possible. Good-bye, my dear. Pray for children."

Later the same day

19 *Monday, February 23, 1987 6:00-6:40 P.M.*

"An Apostolate Of Motherhood"

Vision of Our Blessed Mother:

Blessed Mother: "Continue to pray for all priests as they need your prayers right now.

"The Christ Child will be your guide in perfecting you in the way of motherhood, such a sublime vocation which has sadly fallen into disregard among many. He will help you to understand the beauty and wonder of innocent children. Pray to Him and He will help you. Children are so special to God. Their nurturing is of the utmost importance to Him. He wishes you to do this well.

"I wish all mothers could know and understand this, the importance and sublimity of their vocation. The children which God has given them must be first in their lives, even at times coming before their husbands, but, of course, never before God Himself. The more that you love God, the more you will love your husband and your children. This is a mystery of God's grace and love which you would be unable to understand even if it were explained to you. It is difficult for many to understand this, but if they pray, especially the Rosary, they will begin to understand. Pray the Rosary always, it will help you to understand many things.

"I am sorrowful that so many mothers neglect their duty for other things. This is often unnecessary and solely for the purpose of accumulating more wealth, when their true wealth, their children, go unattended. I pity these poor mothers on their judgment day as they will have much to account for.

"An apostolate of motherhood will grow out of these writings, which will be an apostolate of prayer and duty in the home done in accord with the will of God and for the love of God. This also will be

an aid in my Triumph. *I will be the model for these mothers in their daily lives, and they will imitate my virtues.* This is necessary to combat the tide of evil which has swept across families and destroyed so many homes.

"Pray for this apostolate to begin. I will let you know how later. Go now and tend to your duties after you finish your Rosary."

20

Tuesday, February 24, 1987
11:15 A.M.

"Follow Me For I Am Meek And Humble Of Heart"

Vision of the Christ Child, wearing a crown:

Christ Child: "My Mother wishes to continue speaking to you. Listen carefully to everything she tells you. I have given her this mission to aid in My salvation of the world. She will employ many of her faithful followers in accomplishing this wonderful task.

"You must be prepared to give completely of yourselves now especially, as the time is so crucial. Hold back nothing for yourselves in service to her and the cause for which she inspires you, that is the Triumph of her Immaculate Heart. This will facilitate the Reign of My Sacred Heart. As Mary was a foreshadow of My glory when I came to earth, so she will again be the precursor to My age of love and peace which she foretold at Fatima.

"Many do not fully comprehend the importance of the message of Fatima. This is partially due to the wickedness of men, and to the active suppression of the message by the evil one who would have people believe that My intervention in the affairs of humans does not occur. Direct intervention also in the mystical sense has always occurred throughout the ages because I have willed it to be so. This is to aid in the salvation of many who would otherwise be lost. It is most necessary now due to the wickedness of this generation upon the earth.

"Many have turned their backs to that which is holy, often making a mockery of that which belongs to God. How this grieves Me! I can take no more. This is why I have sent My Mother to you, to instruct you in all My ways and to bring you back to Me. I adjure you to listen to all that she tells you so that her holy mission may be accomplished on the face of the earth.

She, the Spouse of the Holy Spirit, beckons you to follow Me in all My ways.

"Follow Me for I am meek and humble of heart. Remember this always. It will help you to be more like Me. Meek and humble of heart, the beauty of the words alone should inspire you to greater holiness.

"See how loving My Mother is towards you. She is indeed your Mother also. Follow her example as she leads you ever closer to Me. I wish you all to be with Me for eternity. This is the purpose for which I created you—eternal bliss with your heavenly Creator. Turn from sin and come back to Me, to your heavenly home which is prepared for you. Eye has not seen nor ear has heard what God has prepared for those who love Him. Now go in peace."

Vision of the Blessed Mother:

Blessed Mother: "My Son has told you to listen carefully to my words. It is wise for you to do so as it will be helpful in aiding many in accomplishing His will. The Child Jesus, the tenderest of all children, has spoken to your heart. Mark His words well in regard to humility, for as love is the queen of all virtues, so humility is the king. This generation lacks the understanding of this. They must learn to be loving and humble towards one another.

"Pray to me for these graces when you say your Rosaries, and I will grant them in abundance so necessary are they now for your salvation and, in fact, the world itself which hangs on the precipice of destruction. You must be humble and loving to each other in all you do in order to combat the tide of evil of pride and sin.

"Learn to forgive each other quickly so as not to hold grudges against one another. So many refuse to forgive. How sad this is. They cannot expect to be forgiven themselves if they will not forgive others. You need to understand this fully and put it into practice.

"I wish to employ the power of the legions of Holy Angels to help and instruct you in all these ways which are God's, for I am the Queen of Angels. They will be highly instrumental in procuring my Triumph. They continue the battle for your souls daily. When they speak to you, often through your conscience, listen to them. They will help you to obey the laws of God and grow in holiness. Pray to the Holy Angels often for guidance and wisdom to do God's will in your daily duties, and they will help you to follow His will.

"Go now and tend to your child. I will speak to you again later."

My son interrupted. It was 12 Noon.

21

Wednesday, February 25, 1987
10:20-11:15 A.M.

"Do Not Delay In Asking For These Graces"

Vision of the Christ Child:

Christ Child: "I want you to do many things now. My Mother will instruct you on My behalf. It is important that you do all that you are told quickly so as not to waste precious time. Souls are falling into Hell daily because there is no one to pray for them and make atonement for their sins. You must make atonement for their sins along with all My faithful followers so as to save these souls.

"I will be asking you to make many sacrifices, but do not fear as your sacrifices will become your joy. See the beauty of the way in which God works, how even a simple sacrifice done in love for Him will bring you great joy. I will grant you the grace, as I will to all who ask of it. It will be most helpful in bringing about the Triumph of My Mother's Immaculate Heart. Do not delay in asking for these graces."

Mariamante: I did so ask.

Christ Child: "There, I am pleased that you have already responded to My request. This is the way you must always be from now on, immediate in response to My requests. If you wish to obtain the heavenly glory which God has planned for all who love Him, make your response to My requests immediately and wholeheartedly. Many delay too long and, therefore, receive less grace because their response is half-hearted. God is not pleased with these delays which are made by those who still seek to do their own will rather than His Divine Will. They delay in order to weigh the consequences of every move they make, fearing they might have to give up something they relish. This is not true love for God; it stems from love of self. Those who wish to follow Me must do so quickly as the apostles responded when I called them. This is partly why I chose them. They did not look back at what they left behind but rather rejoiced in thanksgiving at having been chosen by God. This is the way you must all be now in response to My Mother and I in Our requests.

"Listen carefully when she speaks, for she is revealing many things that you need to know in order to accomplish My will on earth."

One of my children interrupted and Our Lord said:

Christ Child: "Go and tend to the child."

Then He continued:

Christ Child: "O, how I love her. I wish you could love her in fulfillment of My will. This would be to a very great degree, indeed. After the Trinity, she should be loved best of all before all Angels and Saints.

"Be her servant and you will be My servant. Be her child and you will be My child. But if you are her adversary, you likewise will be My adversary. Many who would call themselves Catholic have lost sight of this truth and need to renounce their folly, for that is what it is indeed. They cannot claim Catholicism to be their faith if they renounce the Mother of the very Church I founded. O what folly. O what sadness this causes Me. They deny My Mother her rightful place in her own Church. Pray for these poor souls so misguided and unenlightened. By their own malice toward her they cut themselves out of the Kingdom of Heaven. Pray that God may have mercy on their souls and enlighten them before they die, as they are doing great damage to My Church by their folly. As the Christ Child, Myself, I adjure them to repent of this grave sin before it is too late for them. Listen now to what My Mother has to tell you."

Mariamante: "Oh Mother, please help me to relate everything correctly."

Blessed Mother: "I will.

"Be kind to your children. This is of the utmost importance. They need your undivided attention when they are small. Mothers should spend more time with the children than they are in many homes. Search your consciences. If you are one of them, correct this. Your children are your jewels, your wealth; guard them as the treasures which they are.

"The priests who neglect their flock are likewise in error. Recreation is not an important aspect of the Christian life and indeed is not in accord with the way of perfection of which I want all my children to trod.[17] They must renounce the selfishness that causes them to waste great amounts of time when souls go unattended in need of the sacraments, particularly Confession. Many of my children are unable to confess their sins due to this. They cannot find a priest who is willing to spend his time in administering this most holy sacrament.

"How sad this is for me to see. The purpose of the priesthood is the administering of the sacraments. Why have they forgotten this? They need to rearrange their priorities and tend to their flock entrusted to them by my Son Himself. Follow His example while on earth. Did He spend needless hours in recreation? Of course not, then why should you if you profess to follow Him and are called to the perfection which is His will for you. The administering of the sacraments of the Holy Eucharist and Penance should be the foremost importance in their lives. Nothing else should take precedence over this ever. Follow this advice and my Son will grant you many graces and make you perfect indeed.

"That is all for now. Go and tend to your duties with joy. I love you."

22

Thursday, February 26, 1987
4:45-5:35 P.M.

"In The Daily Duty. . .Sanctification Will Take Place"

Vision of Our Blessed Mother, wearing a white veil over her head and across her shoulders:

Blessed Mother: "The mercy of God is so great it encompasses all who call upon Him in faith. When you are ever in doubt, call upon the mercy of God, and He will enlighten you.

"Some persons think that they must face great trials in order to be made holy, but it is often in the daily duty that the sanctification will take place. Those who are closest to you will often cause the greatest trials; but take heart as this will not last long.

---

17. I understood this to mean if there is neglect of duty involved or an excess of recreation. This sentence was meant to be taken in context with the rest of the paragraph.—Mariamante.

"You must be attentive to your duty and thereby work out your sanctification. Seeking to do great things in the worldly sense cannot accomplish this. The sanctification of the soul is the work of God with the cooperation and willingness of the individual. He has chosen the path for you and you must follow it in order to accomplish this, His will for you on earth.

"Great things are accomplished in the secrets of the soul when an individual is willing to cooperate fully with God's grace, and with one who is truly abandoned to the will of God. If you understand this, you will know the secret of sanctification. It is quite simple and need not be made complicated. Many confuse greatness in the ways of the world with greatness in sanctification, whereas the two do not necessarily go hand in hand and are often contrary to one another.

"The silence and obscurity of the cloistered life is one of my great joys, to see so many souls serving God for Himself alone and seeking nothing in return from the world. They do not seek greatness in this life, but in the next they shall wear the crown of glory. Follow their example in this regard."

Mariamante: "I wish only to please God, Mother."

Blessed Mother: "Then do all that I tell you and you will. They[18] need your attention more often. You are wise not to talk on the phone so much. A mother must be available to her children when they need her and not busy about other less important things. Your husband must be made to feel needed and important. Help him to have greater respect for himself and others. Kindness will accomplish this. Be careful not to let him feel left out."

Mariamante: "How do I accomplish this, Mother?"

Blessed Mother: "In the little ways of day-to-day living. The television has become an intrusion into the modern home. Its influence has not always been good and is leading many astray due to a faulty value system. Turn it off when it is not appropriate and do not watch what is not befitting a Catholic home. Do not let yourselves be brainwashed in effect by the faulty values of a few who influence this media to the detriment of the whole society it effects.

---

18. The children.—Mariamante.

"Stand up for what is right. Do not be silent in the face of wrong. Let your Christian values permeate the society around you. If you wish to have a greater effect on those around you for the glory of God, then be holy yourselves. This is the only way this will come about. I hope that my words will not fall upon deaf ears of the mothers who need them, for they have the greatest influence in their homes in regard to morality. Use this influence to further the cause of purity and holiness, and not only will your families be blessed by God but all who are around you. They will taste and see the goodness of the Lord and wish to follow Him. That is all."

I was wondering why there were so many answers to things in my own life, when she responded:

Blessed Mother: "This is because I wish to speak to other mothers through you and your everyday living experiences.

"Always be truthful and you will never go wrong."

I asked her to help my husband for whom I had offered up this day. She said:

Blessed Mother: "I will."

Mariamante: "Thank you, Mother."

23

Friday, February 27, 1987
Approximately 10:00 A.M.

St. Joseph

A silent vision of Our Lord as an adult at ______ Catholic Church. Also a private message regarding my family and having to do with St. Joseph and the Christ Child.

24

Sunday, March 1, 1987
11:25 A.M.

"Go To Confession Frequently"

Vision of Our Blessed Mother:

Blessed Mother: "My child, do not fear. The enemy is indeed harassing you. I will not let him harm you though he may try. This is due to the mission for which you have been chosen. He wishes to suppress it because it is my cause. Your children too are being harassed although I will not let them be harmed in any way. Your husband has nearly succumbed to the tyranny. Continue to pray for him.

"My adversary does not want this message to be revealed. He will continue to try to suppress it. You must be aware of this. Tell this to Father so that he also will be aware. Nearly everyone working for my cause, the Triumph, will be experiencing some harassment now in accord with the importance of their mission for which I have entrusted them. Do not fear this. Consider it part of your sanctification. Invoke my aid and protection in these times and I will continue to protect you.

"Father must understand this and continue to bless you and your home. This will be of great help in combating the wiles of the evil one. He fears the holy priests and their blessings. They crush his power. Continue in your daily duty also in the midst of these episodes. This also will be of help. Remain in holy obedience and you have nothing to fear. Never forget this.

"My Child Jesus has infuriated the enemy from the time of His birth. The fact that a child in human flesh has snatched away his kingdom and brought salvation to the world enrages him. His fury knows no bounds and continues to be unleashed upon the followers of my Son. Jesus crushed his power by the Cross. By the Cross you shall also conquer all evil.

"My Son loves you so; He will not let a hair on your head be harmed, though try as they may. Invoke the protection of the Precious Blood. Fear nothing but sin and displeasing God. Confess your sins openly. This will confound the enemy's wiles. He wants all to lack the self-knowledge which comes from confessing your sins openly and without fear of human respect. Your sins are few, but many of my children are steeped in sin due to their refusal to use this holy sacrament instituted by my Son.

"I wish all my children would make use of this sacrament and go to Confession frequently, not sporadically or seldom. Frequent, regular Confession will make them grow in holiness in a way in which nothing else can. Pray for those who neglect or fear the confessional. They must overcome this in order to grow closer to my Divine Son. May He be praised now and for eternity. I will protect you in all circumstances. Go now in peace. Your Mother loves you."

25

Monday, March 2, 1987
10:30-11:47 A.M.

"Seek Only To Love Me"

Vision of the Blessed Mother, followed by the Christ Child:

Blessed Mother: "Your time may not be as limited as you think. I will give you all the time which is necessary to complete my mission. This I will arrange as I explained before, when your family does not require your attention.

"I have arranged for Father ______ to be in this area, your vicinity, as you know. I want you to go see him. Do ask for his blessing as you had planned. He is one of my special sons who is accomplishing a great task for me. Your task will be similar in nature to his, although you will not be in the public eye as he has been. This is part of my plan to protect you and your family who would not be able to understand all that is occurring. For this reason I have chosen to keep you anonymous. You can be most thankful for this as many have not enjoyed such great anonymity. . .They suffered much from exposure to the public who can be very cruel. I do not wish for you to endure this suffering and so I shall continue to protect your privacy.

"My Son has told you to listen carefully to me. Now listen to Him as He reveals a mystery, a secret of the heart, to you."

Christ Child: "I do not want My children to be overburdened with information which will not aid them in growing closer to Me. I speak of the trend of which you yourself have been concerned. You are correct to have this aversion to evil; it comes directly from Me and is in itself a gift. Many do not understand this and perceive it to be lack of strength; however, abhorrence to all evil should be the norm for all My followers, not just a few.

"Sadly, there is a trend among some who would have you think that being prepared for what may come spiritually, that is in the spiritual realm, to include human knowledge, that is, knowledge which is not truly spiritual in nature. The more information which one accumulates about the evil one and his cohorts does nothing to further their own spiritual development and, in fact, can often hinder it by keeping the focus on that which is not of God.

"The secret of the heart which I wish to reveal to you is this: he who would seek only to love Me and to do all for My glory has no interest in the work of the evil one except to renounce it. A heart full of love for Me has no room for anything else and will show a disinterest in that which is evil. That is not to say that there are not some, such as certain priests who are chosen to act against the evil one as exorcists, but these are few and specially chosen by Me.

"The trend of today's Christian, in being fascinated by the work of the evil one, only exposes the shallowness of their love for Me. They devote their time and energy to a form of shallow sensationalism at the guise of being prepared, when they would do much better to spend this time in prayer or with Me in the Blessed Sacrament. That is how they will be prepared, not by accumulating knowledge of the evil one and his works. His works are many in the world today. Your work should be in combating him through prayer and penance not through knowledge of evil.

"I adjure My followers to take their eyes off the evil one and put them on the things of Heaven. Where your time is spent, there will be your heart; it reveals where the heart truly is. Do not rejoice so much in that you have been given power to cast out demons but in that your names have been written in Heaven.

"The essence of the heart is love. If you truly love Me, you will seek only that which is of Me, not that which is of him who hates Me. Satan himself has worked to perpetrate this folly, giving My children a false sense of security in their so-called knowledge of what is to be. Again I state to you: the best preparation you can have is to be prepared through long hours in prayer, penance done out of love for Me and more time spent with Me in the Blessed Sacrament. This will not only prepare you for any occurrences in this world but also in the next. I will ask of you when I see you face-to-face: How did you spend your time? Did you spend it with Me or with My adversary? How you answer is up to you. Now is the time to make your choice.

"Another aspect which grieves Me about this modern phenomenon is the self-righteousness which often grows out of persons[19] involved in this activity of demon-chasing as it were. They look upon those who have been so sadly misled as somehow inferior to them and become puffed up with pride and self-knowledge. However, if it were not for My grace and mercy they would surely be the same. What have you to glory in? Is not all God's? Is not all My creation? Is not all My knowledge? There is no room for pride or self-glory among those who profess to love Me. They must love all My creatures, yes, even those who have fallen into sin. This is how they will be helped. They will see your love for Me and others and wish to be like you. The holiness I give you will convert others, will bring others fallen far from Me, back to Me if you are truly My witness on earth.

"So I say to you again, if you truly love Me, spend your time with Me, all your time; do not divide your time which is rightfully Mine with the work of the evil one. Let him be forgotten and obscure, not in the forefront of your mind. Renounce him and his works, that is enough to say of him, and spend your thoughts, your time, your love on Me and My works.

"Follow the example of the Saints in this. They spoke little of the evil one but always of Me and My Mother and that which is holy. Amen I say to you, he who truly professes to love Me will renounce all that is of this world including its prince of darkness and follow Me.

"Follow Me for I am meek and humble of heart. Only seek the knowledge of the things of God that will bring you closer to Me, not the things of the evil one.

"Do not be frightened. Rejoice in that you have been chosen by Me to give this message to the world. Do not be concerned about human respect. This could become your downfall if you are not careful. Seek only to please Me and not man. Human respect is fleeting and ever changing. My love for you remains the same today as yesterday and for tomorrow. Sing praise to your Heavenly Creator. This is how I wish you to spend your time, with Me. Go now and tend to your daily duty in peace.

---

19. Pious souls who show undue interest in the work of the evil one. —Mariamante.

"If you wonder why I am addressing your concerns, it is because they are My concerns; in fact, I have given them to you. You are beginning to see things ever more clearly. This is a direct result of your being brought closer to Me by Myself and through My Mother's intercession. It is she who has chosen you to be My bride. She will prepare you for the wedding feast. Listen to her and follow her example. Go now as I tell you."

26

Tuesday, March 3, 1987
3:10-4:10 P.M.

"Do Not Fight The Cross, Rather Accept It"

Vision of the Christ Child:

Christ Child: "Continue to pray for purity in the world. It is necessary now.

"You are experiencing the rage of the enemy but it will soon pass. This was a great trial for your family, but I will not allow it to continue. It will soon leave your home. The serpent's back was crushed long ago so you need not fear him. He is powerless to those who love Me. You have fared well throughout this trial. I hope others will do the same when put to the test. It is not always easy, I know, but by faith you will conquer all adversity. Trust in Me alone and the intercessory power of My Mother and there is nothing under Heaven that can truly harm you."

Mariamante: "Lord, please help Mrs. _____.[20] And my husband."[21]

Christ Child: "I will. You must remember these visions and their messages are meant for others, not only yourself."

Mariamante: "Yes, Lord. Little Lord Jesus, I love you and hope I didn't do anything wrong."

Christ Child: "No, but keep this in mind when you are asking questions. I want you to know that all who love Me have nothing to fear. Fear is useless, what is needed is trust. Moral courage and patience are very necessary in this age."

At this point there were several interruptions by my children when He responded:

---

20. A lady who was in a car accident.—Mariamante.
21. Whom I was concerned about.—Mariamante.

Christ Child: "You need not worry about interruptions. I understand all of this.

"You will soon endure a test of faith that will be most difficult. It will try you to the soul, but the fruits will be most beautiful. This is the way it must be. Purification must precede any spiritual growth in order for it to be valid. You must understand this and remember it in the times of trial. They are only temporary, not everlasting like My love for you. In times of trial think of the love of God and this will be your comfort. He has not forgotten you and never will. Rejoice that you have been chosen to suffer in a similar fashion as I did. This is a most beautiful gift and one I bestow on few of My children. Keep this in mind over the next few weeks as Lent begins.

"I will help you to understand more as time goes on but not always in the same way. You must be prepared to suffer greatly, but My Mother will also comfort you and We will never leave you, though at times it may seem so. You would not be able to understand all of this now even if I explained it to you because it requires the purification of the soul to understand the things of God.

"Rejoice in your trials; they are setting you free from the bonds of slavery to sin. Sin in various degrees, even minor sins, are highly offensive to God. All sin must be purified from the soul before a soul can stand before the throne of God in Heaven. If you wish for this to occur to you while on earth, you must be prepared to suffer in this life at least somewhat in order to merit the Kingdom of Heaven, some to greater and some to lesser degrees depending upon the individual soul and the will of God.

"You must soon prepare for Confession. I want you to continue going to Confession frequently. This is the least difficult means of purification, suffering, of course, being the most difficult. But as I told you before, even your suffering will be turned to joy if united to Mine.

"You may ask why is there so much suffering in the world today: because there is so much sin. The expiation of sin can be a difficult task if the soul resists purification, but if he sees the merit in suffering, uniting it to Mine on the Cross, he will begin to see clearly. This clarity in itself then aids the person in their suffering, giving it the meaning that is necessary to aid in redemption.

"Many suffer blindly, not understanding its value. This is unfortunate. They need not feel the aloneness that accompanies this kind of suffering if they were to turn to Me and unite their suffering with Mine. My Passion will give them strength and peace and they will no longer resist the cross.

"Do not fight the cross, rather accept it as the glory it truly is. This is difficult for you to understand in your nature but you will begin to understand in time. Most of My children now have very little understanding of this. This is why I wish to emphasize it by repeating it often.

"Fear nothing that unites you to Me, such as your trials and crosses, rather fear only that which separates you from Me such as pleasures and indulgences of the flesh. Pray for strength and courage to carry your crosses, not to have them taken away when they are your means of purification or sanctification.

"Although the mercy of God indeed includes the cures of many afflictions, it is only in those cases where I deem it as unnecessary for their salvation to carry that particular cross. If a cross or trial is of great spiritual value, I will not remove it, and you should never wish that it were, for it may be the means of salvation of many not only the individual soul.

"Remember My words throughout this Lent, and remember that I love you beyond your understanding as I do all My dear children. Praise the Holy Trinity."

27

Thursday, March 5, 1987
9:20-10:10 P.M.

"Respond Now With Your Fiat"

Vision of Our Blessed Mother and the Christ Child:

Blessed Mother: *"I wish for the apostolate of motherhood to begin very soon.* This will aid in my Triumph because it will include many mothers who will rise to holiness through this means. They will learn to offer up their daily duty in a most efficacious way and help to atone for much of the sin in the world. They will learn to use their time wisely, and it will be well spent in prayer, not superficial or superfluous prayer, but prayer that will pierce the Heart of my Son because of its genuineness and love.

"They will love their children and their husbands and their homes above all else except God and myself, and they will be shining examples to all those around them. Their interest will be in the home, and they will not seek to aspire to anything except perfection in this most noble way. They will put their children far before themselves and all others, and they will love their husbands deeply in a holy Christian love.

"They will love the Church and seek to do all for the salvation of souls and my Triumph. They will work for peace by their example and prayer, but not through activism which would detract from the purity of their vocation to which I am calling them. They must be self-sacrificing examples and models of love and kindness to all whom they meet.

"My Son wishes to speak to you."

Christ Child: "My Mother has instructed you of this apostolate that she wishes you to begin. This will also aid in the mitigation of the suffering of children which I spoke to you about earlier. This will aid in this by the growth in holiness of so many individuals that they will aid in stemming the tide of evil, of which I spoke earlier, and will help many children who would otherwise suffer much. This is why it will be your joy.

"I am pleased that you said yes to My request before you knew what it entailed. This shows the generous heart which I want all My children to have when I make requests of them. Many do not know that it is often in very simple tasks that I request things of them. Many hesitate when I ask things of them. Never hesitate when your God asks something of you. Always trust in Him and answer yes immediately, even as My Mother did when she responded with the famous fiat which brought Me into the world.

"I will always give you the grace you need to accomplish any task or else I would not ask it of you. This you must believe deeply so that when you respond in faith, it will be wholehearted. I know that many of My children are frightened of the extraordinary and wish for all to continue in a mundane and ordinary way, but this is not always the will of God. You must respond to the will of God whatever it may be. To say no to your Creator is to deny Him what is rightfully due Him, that is, your undying love manifested in service to Him and others, and intense prayer for yourselves and the world.

"Oh, pray for the world especially now when it is so urgent! The cries of the innocent call out to Me. So much injustice cannot continue for long. It must be changed and very soon or a grave chastisement will come to all the world; this is the way it must be. Heaven can tolerate no more. My Father and I have determined it so. Either change or this will have to come about.

"My Mother's intercession will aid you in all your needs. You need not fear anything. Call on her in all circumstances and she will aid you, even to bringing many of you to great heights of holiness which is so necessary right now. I say to all who read this: Respond now with your fiat and let it be wholehearted so that you will aid in the Triumph of My Mother, which will be the salvation of the world in this generation and the era of peace of which she spoke at Fatima. Now is the time. Do not delay. Tomorrow is no more. I wish all My children to understand the importance of this immediate response to My Mother and My requests. They are simple and easily accomplished by My grace. They need not fear any extraordinary burdens who call upon My Name. I will give them all the graces necessary to accomplish all things, even easily if you have faith. *Faith can change the world.* Have faith in Me and My Mother's intercession and let the world be changed.

"Pray for children and this apostolate to begin. It will be very holy and pleasing to Me because it will be the work of My Mother, who does all things for her Creator and the children she loves. Amen I say to you, you can never be thankful enough for what God has done for you in giving you this tender and beautiful Mother who makes recompense for your sins. Pray to God in thanksgiving for her. He is pleased with this prayer from your hearts.

"That is all for now. Continue to transcribe and give your papers to Father quickly. There is not much time.

"I bless you all from My Heart."

28

Saturday, March 7, 1987
12:00-1:05 P.M.

"The Answer To All Modern Day Woes Is In The Sacraments..."

Vision of the Christ Child, then Our Blessed Mother:

Christ Child: "I wish to begin My discourse today on the need for modesty in dress and in all facets of modern day life. This lack of appropriate dress has become most distressing to Me and My Mother who is the model of all purity. She should be your guide and example to follow in this. I want young women to be modest in their dress, and I want their parents to enforce this. Parents themselves have grown slack in this area of discipline and allow that which is totally improper for My children. Guide your children in the proper standards by setting them yourselves and instructing and admonishing them when necessary. Parents of even a generation or two ago would never have allowed what is tolerated today.

"I also wish to address the problem of children who are directly led astray by their parents' poor example. This is sadly very common now, and one I wish to curb through the apostolate I spoke of before. There are many instances where mothers, in particular, have become bad examples for their children in regard to purity and modesty in dress and practice. They have illicit relationships which damage the home almost beyond repair. But if they turn to Me, I will restore them to grace and purity if they repent of their sins.

"The fathers of this generation have become as children themselves, seeking only pleasure and childish forms of recreation. They need to be serious-minded and mature examples for their children, not playmates to them. Children need to learn respect for authority; but how can this be if their own fathers act as children seeking only to indulge their pleasures.

"The tragedy in modern society is that parents no longer wish to be parents; they want to be children themselves. What a shame! What a pity! Their children have no one to look up to because their parents lack the moral fortitude to combat even the simplest forms of temptation and sin. The only way they will gain this strength, which was so apparent even in times not long ago, is through prayer and remorse for their sins. They must repent of their sins.

"They must seek Me in the sacraments of Holy Mother Church who is their supreme guide to holiness on earth. The Church I have founded is their answer. *The answer to all modern day woes is in the sacraments of My Church.* It is an everlasting gift of My love to you, the path so clear and yet so often unchosen. It need not be unchosen for you, if you turn to Me in the holy Sacrament of Penance. I will give you the strength to be all that I wish you would be, if you turn to Me and be cleansed of your sins in this way.

"You defile yourselves with unworthy Communions after mortal sins have been committed. This is an outrage and must be stopped. Do not go to Communion with mortal sin on your soul. It is a grave sin in itself to do this. My priests need to express this more clearly and more often, as many have totally forgotten this teaching. Yet, most who do this are still culpable, because they know of this teaching yet prefer to ignore it. They have reduced the thought of sin in their minds to practically nothing at all, convincing themselves that serious or mortal sin is nearly impossible to commit. I say to you this day, that this is a grave and serious error which you must overcome, if you wish to enter the Kingdom of Heaven which I have prepared for you. You will not enter with mortal sin on your souls. You have cut yourselves off from My grace by your actions and will not be allowed to set foot in My Father's house.

"This grieves Me greatly, but you must be the ones to repent and stop piling error on top of error. The confessionals should be full of those seeking My grace and mercy. Do not hesitate; go today, even as you read this so that you will not be one held accountable for these sins and errors. I do not wish to see you perish in eternal fire, but you separate yourselves from Me by your obstinacy in sin and refusal to repent. Rise above the standards of this world and do what you know is right in your hearts without waiting for tomorrow to come.

"Today is the day the Lord has made, let us rejoice and be glad. Use your time wisely, as you may never know when it will be your day to account for all that you have done in your life, that is, your individual day of judgment, your death on this earth.

"My Mother has more instructions for you and for Father so listen carefully to her now."

Blessed Mother: "My Son has chosen you for this apostolate. Continue to pray for its inception. I do not want Father to delay for a great amount of time, as I wish for this apostolate to begin very quickly as I have stated before. He must understand the need to get this information to those whom I wish to have it, that is, the everyday persons not only in this country but many countries around the world. They will understand my words when they read them, and it will inspire them because it is my work, not the work of human hands, but mine in the glorified state united to my Son for the glory of the Most Holy Trinity.

"We wish to help the families of the earth floundering in sin and error which has become so rampant, and is choking off their very life; and threatens the very existence of the family at all in some countries such as yours. As you know, Satan has targeted the family and the priesthood because these are the holiest of vocations from which most of my children come to me in Heaven. Sadly, many children are not even born into families today, but are orphaned even before their birth by the choice of their parents who do not want them. This grieves my Heart so. Cherish your children and give them the stable environment they deserve.

"Cast off the mentality of the world which says you must indulge your own whims, and sacrifice for your families. This is true love, when manifested in sacrifice. Luxuries are not important; they could be your ruin. Do not seek material wealth. It is of no importance and can often be detrimental to your coming to my Son. Forget the things of earth and seek the things of Heaven, that which is everlasting, so that when you are to account for all, you can rejoice that you have done well with your time on earth. You need not be scrupulous in every detail, just live a good life, as the teachings of the Church dictate.

"This is simple and easy enough to accomplish by the grace of God, Who provides for you in all your necessities. He has made it easy for you through the institution of the most holy sacraments of the Catholic Church; but you must use them to benefit from them, or they can do you no good.

"I adjure you all who read this. Cast off the darkness of sin and put on the armor of light which is my Son Jesus Christ, Who comes to you in the sacraments of your Church, the Holy

Catholic Church. Follow the example of the Holy Father who instructs you wisely in all things, and the Magisterium, which is the teaching arm of the Church. Do this and you will attain the Kingdom of Heaven.

"I pray for you all to open your hearts to my Son, and I am praying for your repentance. Listen to Him now before it is too late for you personally, that is, each one of you.

"I must go now. I will speak to you again later."

Mariamante: "Mother, I love you."

Blessed Mother: "And I love you."

29

Sunday, March 8, 1987
10:30-11:15 A.M.

"Obedience To The Magisterium"

Vision of the Christ Child:

Christ Child: "The aspect of My Passion which you are enduring now is the Agony in the Garden. Tell this to Father. . .

"I am saddened by what is happening in this area in the Church: They are not being obedient to My precepts as laid down by the Magisterium of the Church. The bond which I solidified for them when they became priests was obedience to the Magisterium and its teaching authority. The confusion of today stems from lack of understanding or following through with this union, which I made for them. They need fear nothing but sin itself.

"The individual bishops have no authority to override this teaching body in even the smallest or what may seem insignificant way. Because, indeed, nothing is insignficant when it pertains to the matters which they address, that is, matters of the most sacred mysteries of My Church. All is important in this light. Though some would have you think that there are aspects which can be tampered with or changed to some greater or lesser degrees, I state emphatically that this is not the case and never will be. All that is set forth by the Magisterium is of the utmost importance, particularly that which directly applies to the administration of My sacraments, which must be done properly and in accord with the specifics as explained by the Holy Father, who is My representative on earth, and this authority and teaching body of the Church, the Magisterium. I wish to make this very clear so as to end the confusion which My loyal priests are suffering from. They need not suffer from the interior confusion and pain if they remember this."

At this point, there were several interruptions by my son, when the Christ Child said:

"It is all right. Tend to the child. Remember it is in your daily duty that you are sanctified."

Then He continued:

Christ Child: "Try to remain calm in the midst of all adversity. If you can maintain your peace throughout your trials, it will be of great help to you. Be attentive when I am speaking to you. Keep your soul at peace and your conscience clear. It is true there may be times when it will seem almost impossible to do so, and that is truly when you are experiencing My Passion; but remember you are suffering in union with Me and for the salvation of many souls, and you will have the perspective which is necessary to maintain your peace.

"I cannot emphasize enough the importance of maintaining a clear conscience in this regard. It will give you peace in the midst of this suffering. You are correct in having thought this. I know that it is not easy but My strength will sustain you. It is not easy to stand alone in the face of that which is wrong, but do not forget that I suffered at the hands of the chief priests and Pharisees. It was they who coerced Pilate into his decision to allow Me to be crucified. In fact, he was initially unwilling to do so, but was pressured to do that which is wrong even though he knew it to be so. Do not be like him in even the smallest way. Do not deny Me or the laws I have set forth for your own good and the good of My people.

"You must be shining examples of truth as I have set forth, shining examples of purity and obedience to the true teaching authority of the Church. I know that many of you are suffering greatly now in this regard, but be strong, stand firm, and be stouthearted and wait for the Lord, and I will deliver you from all evil, including that evil which is hidden in the hearts of many who themselves do not even know it. They are the ones who can and are doing the most damage to My Church, the ones who profess to speak the truth but in reality are espousing lies. They will have much to account for when their time comes, as they are leading many away from the truth by their errors.

"In some areas the true faith is no longer being practiced due to this modern phenomenon of selective practice of My truths and teachings. They choose only what they wish to understand and deny that the other teachings exist. Pray for them. They need your prayers. It is by your prayers and sufferings that their conversion will come about.

"That is all for now..."

Mariamante: "Little Lord Jesus, please help my husband."

Christ Child: "I will. I have already begun to do so as you can see. He is still resisting but the worst is past."

Mariamante: "Thank you, Lord."

Christ Child: "Pray the rest of your Rosary for priests today."

30

Monday, March 9, 1987
11:00-11:30 A.M.

"Prayer Is Your Answer"

Vision of the Christ Child:

Christ Child: "As you can see, the difficulties and obstacles of getting to Me in the Blessed Sacrament are becoming greater all the time. *This is a direct result of the lack of love manifested to Me in the Blessed Sacrament.* The churches being locked even during the day now has made it increasingly difficult for My children who do truly love Me in this Most Blessed Sacrament to come to Me. How sad this is. There would be no need to lock the churches if they were full as they should be now in these times of crisis and evil.

"Turn to Me rather than each other in times of crisis. Persons spend hours talking about their problems to each other, when if they spent half that time with Me in the Blessed Sacrament, all their problems would be solved. I say solved in the sense of them having strength to carry their crosses or, in some cases, even removed if it is not for the betterment of their soul that they carry it. Many carry needless burdens because they do not come to Me. They seek human solutions when there are none.

"I alone can truly help you. You must learn this in time if you are to be truly Mine and not of this world. Why all this talk in the face of problems? Prayer is your answer, not talking to each other repeatedly about the same things. The modern phenomenon of a group to meet every need is not necessary if you truly love Me and come to Me in all your afflictions. In many cases, these groups even hinder the spiritual growth of My children by making them dependent on these programs and people rather than Me and My Mother.

"God alone can truly help you in the way in which you need it, and My Mother's intercession will make it all possible. Turn to her in your needs and sorrows. Tell her your woes, not each other. Pray for help and guidance. Think of others and pray for the world. This will give you the peace and joy you seek. Idle talk, idle hours spent in useless talk is unnecessary and can often be dangerous for the soul. When will My children learn this! They seek answers in each other, when they have none. I alone have the answers to peace of mind and heart.

"The turmoil which plagues this generation, robbing them of their inner peace is caused from sin itself, sin in all its manifestations. Unconfessed sin will rob you of your peace. Go to Confession. Visit Me in the Blessed Sacrament and pray to My Mother, especially her Rosary, and you will have peace. And if you seriously wish to come to Me, be wholehearted in your response to Me and My requests. I will give you the peace and joy which surpasses all understanding. Pray for peace in the world, peace of heart, peace of mind, peace of soul, and you will indeed have peace in the world. It will start in your own hearts.

"My Mother has told you the way at Fatima, re-emphasizing My Gospel message. Listen to her, follow the Gospel life; thrust your needless cares away and trust in Me and My Mother. We will accomplish great things in you if you allow Us, but you must be willing. Pray for willing spirits to do the will of My Father and it will be granted to you. But again, you must pray for this, as it is a most beautiful and precious thing that must be asked for. As you know, prayer is the prerequisite that God has set forth for all that is to be granted to you in the spiritual realm.

"Ask and it shall be given to you, seek and you shall find, knock and it shall be opened to you. Do this and you shall receive, nay even in abundance. Ask for the virtues of My Mother, the seven gifts of the Holy Spirit and they will be granted to you. Amen I say to you, *the Kingdom of Heaven belongs to those who pray*. Pray and you shall attain it. Pray and you shall obtain more than your hearts now imagine in their smallness. I bless you all from My Heart."

31

Tuesday, March 10, 1987
6:00-6:30 P.M.

"Contemplative And Mental Prayer"

Vision of the Christ Child:

Christ Child: "Continue to pray the Stations of the Cross throughout Lent, and throughout the year, if possible, particularly on Fridays. These traditional devotions are most pleasing to Me and My Father. The need for intense prayer is ever increasing, so much so that I wish all My dear children to spend most of their days in this most efficacious fashion for the salvation of souls.

"This will not be difficult for those who have mastered the practice of mental or contemplative prayer. Many of My children do not understand this beautiful form of prayer which is more pleasing to Me than the mere recital of words. My Saints understood this and practiced this form of prayer throughout their days. In fact, once a soul finds the joy in this form of prayer, it may be difficult for them to continue in vocal prayer.

"Although the Rosary is a necessity for My children, particularly now in these turbulent times, I wish for My children to do much more in the way of prayer. They should be spending literally hours in prayer for the world, according to their station in life. If you understand contemplative prayer and practice mental prayer throughout your day, you will be in union with Me as you do your daily duty. This is how I want you to be—living prayer-filled existences.

"I cannot stress enough the importance of this for those who wish to attain the perfection of which is My Father's and of which I spoke while on earth. Be perfect even as your Heavenly Father is perfect. I will aid you in this, even in the smallest attempt made by a soul. Your God is a generous God. He wishes all that is good for you, but you must be willing and cooperative with the grace in order to accomplish these things. Do not resist My will for you.

"Those of you who are housewives will find that contemplative and mental prayer are well suited to your station in life. Many laymen in the work place will also find this most compatible with their occupations, particularly those involved in manual or physical labor. You need not think of this form of prayer being suitable only for those in monasteries or convents. It is for all My children who are willing to practice it. Spiritual direction is another aspect of your life which you must pursue if you wish to attain this perfection, of course, which is made possible by My grace. Seek out holy priests to guide you in this path. They will be of great help to you.

"I hope that many of you will learn to follow this path very soon as My graces are now being poured forth upon the earth and are yours for the asking. My Mother's intercession is so powerful that whatever you ask of her will be granted almost immediately, if it be for the benefit of your soul, aids in holiness, and for the glory of God. Do all for the glory of God Who loves you so.

"Tend to your children and I will speak to you again later. My Mother also wishes to speak to you later. Go now."

32

Later same day
Tuesday, March 10, 1987 6:40 P.M.

"My Mission"

Vision of Our Blessed Mother, wearing a white veil:

Blessed Mother: "In regard to Father, I know that he is having many difficulties now, but he must not let these stand in the way of my mission to which I am entrusting him. He must understand that this is to be the priority in his life now because it is I myself who am calling him to it. He must set other less important things aside now for this to take precedence. I want to stress the importance of this so that he will be zealous in accomplishing the task for which I am calling him forth. This may at times seem difficult, but all things that are of importance are at times difficult. This adds to their merit.

"I want him to make the necessary effort soon to contact those whom I have already instructed him. He will need to do this in order to begin this project. I understand the difficulties of daily life, but I would not give any of my children a task which they could not accomplish.

"Go now and contact Father tonight."

33

Friday, March 13, 1987
9:10-9:45 A.M.

"Love My Mother And You Will Love Me"

Vision of the Christ Child:

Christ Child: "With My Mother all is eternal springtime. You will learn this more and more as time goes on. She has created for you a veritable paradise in her Heart. Go to her when she calls you. Follow her inspirations. She will always lead you to Me. I know that many hesitate to call upon My Mother, fearing it will somehow detract from their love for Me. How foolish this is. They do not understand the meaning of love. They would never think this if they understood My nature. I am never jealous of My Mother because it is I Who have planned for her to intercede for you. It is My expressed wish that it be this way. As I told you before some years ago: 'In Heaven there is no jealousy,' and 'Souls are not worthy to come to Me first; they must go through her Immaculate Heart.' I hope that many will read this and put the nonsense behind them that has been perpetrated by her adversary, the evil one. Never be afraid to turn to My Mother in all circumstances. She should be the one to whom you go and who will lead you to Me.

"*When a soul is united to My Mother and firmly ensconced in her Heart, I can refuse them nothing, they are so pleasing to Me.* They are made pleasing by her intercession which purifies them of this world and fashions them after Me, even as I was fashioned in her womb by the power of the Holy Spirit. But again, *she* was necessary for the plan of the Incarnation to be fulfilled, so she is necessary for your personal redemption, or coming to Me. She is the Gate of Heaven by which I have come to you and you will come to Me. The protestantism that has crept into My Church, that is the one I founded, the Catholic Church, is just that—protestantism. It is not Catholic truth. It is an error to diminish the importance of My Mother's role in your salvation and the salvation of the world. She was and is most important in all facets of redemption because I chose to come to you by this means and I choose for you to come to Me by the same means, that is the Blessed Virgin Mary, My Mother and your Mother.

"She is Queen of all Saints, Queen of Angels, and Queen of Heaven and Earth. She will lead you to Heaven if you allow her. I am grieved by so much resistance to My Mother's message both here and at Fatima and so many of her apparitions. She is pleading for your souls and your cooperation but so many turn a deaf ear. They need to rearrange the priorities in their lives so that the things of Heaven are of the utmost importance to them rather than secondary in their lives. When she speaks to you listen and learn for it is My will that she has come to you and is speaking to you. If you reject her message, you reject Me because it is I Who have sent her.

"Remember this well. It is your warning: My Mother is to be well received in your hearts or I shall not allow you to set foot in My kingdom. Those who would think she is somehow expendable are in grave error and need to rethink their position. Their obstinacy in this matter must be amended so that they can love fully as I have planned for all creatures to love. Love My Mother and you will love Me as My Father planned.

"Go now and prepare more papers for Father. My Mother will speak to you again later. I love you and bless you from My Heart."

34

Saturday, March 14, 1987
12:20 P.M.

"Trust Only In Me And My Mother"

Vision of the Christ Child:

Christ Child: "I know that you are having difficulty in continuing in your Rosary. This is due to the reason I explained earlier.[22] Do not worry about it but mention it to Father.

"My love dictates that all who are joined to Me rise above the things of this world including the pettiness sometimes manifested in your human natures. I want you all to rise above these imperfections and trust only in Me and My Mother. I will say no more on this subject as I hope it will be already ended.

"The subject I wish to treat today is chastity as a way of life."

At this point, there was a lengthy interruption. Later I was instructed to phone my spiritual director, which I did immediately.

---

22. Experiencing contemplative prayer.—Mariamante.

35

Sunday, March 15, 1987
5:30-6:33 P.M.

"The Beauty Of Chastity"

Vision of the Christ Child:

Christ Child: "The Lord deals out vengeance with a two-edged sword and vengeance is Mine says the Lord. Those who have mutilated their bodies in the never-ending attempt to prevent life are in need of repentance. They have sinned in a grievous manner and should remain chaste in atonement for their sin. Behold the sorrow which this aberration of today's society has caused, particularly to the children who are victims of it, victims in the sense of having all in the material realm but deficient in love due to having no brothers or sisters. The parents who have opted to destroy life even before it has begun have created a void for the few who have survived the stipulations of the modern world's thinking. They suffer from loneliness, lack of filial affection, and in all manner that is manifested directly from this aberration. To deny human life because of the whimsical and precarious excuses of today's person is an outrage against the Divine Order, and is directly responsible for much of the sin and tragedy that you witness today.

"How can human life be compared to material things? That which lacks life is nothing in comparison to that which is eternal, the human soul. Such nonsense! And yet so many have believed it; and more are falling each day to the pressures that this rampant error has caused being out of control, so much so that those in My Own Church are hardly distinguishable from those who lack the truth, by practicing these same hedonistic methods and life styles. For shame! They must repent and soon.

"Chastity is a beautiful practice which frees the heart in a special way to love divinely. I commend those who are having difficulty, those called to such in life, to My Mother who will be their advocate and support in times of trial or temptation. She who was totally pure from the moment of her existence will aid them in many ways and help them overcome any difficulties no matter how great they may seem.

"I have chosen her to be your model in this manner so that this generation, so depraved in these practices of wanton behavior, may rise above the world's standards through her intercession and example. If it were not for her intercession many would be lost now due to the severity of this situation. The immorality has become out of control to the point that all of the society is suffering from it.

"The beauty of chastity and modesty will again be valued during the reign of the Immaculate Heart of My Mother, so that all will see the clarity which this provides in the path to Me and your heavenly home.

"My children are suffering so from these rampant errors in thought and practice, I wish to intervene for them. *They must honor Me in the image of the Sacred Heart* and I will help them to overcome the insidious plagues which are creeping into homes. I speak of plagues in the sense of sin from immorality and immodesty. You will enjoy peace in your homes from this tyranny if you honor Me in this fashion. Protect your homes and your children with the image of Me and My Sacred Heart. Wear the Sacred Heart badge and place My image in a prominent place in your homes, and I will bless you in abundance. Few know or truly understand the power that I have given to this devotion of honoring Me in this fashion. If they knew, they would indeed practice it. I have come to tell you again to use the practices which I have revealed in the past for your salvation and protection. The myriad of devotions which have been handed down through the ages, approved by My Church, should be put into practice and their use widespread to curb the evil which lurks today waiting to devour like a hungry lion any who fall prey. Arm yourselves with holiness and that which is holy, My sacramentals and devotions, so that you will not fall prey. My Mother's Rosary and Scapular and the Sacred Heart's devotion will offer you the most protection and aid in your holiness to a great degree.

"I want all My children to practice the Nine First Friday's[23] *in*

---

23. The traditional devotion to the Sacred Heart includes receiving Holy Communion on nine consecutive first Fridays of the month as an act of reparation to the Sacred Heart. The following are the twelve promises of Our Lord given to St. Margaret Mary Alacoque for those devoted to His Sacred Heart: "1) I will give them all the graces necessary in their state of life. 2) I will establish peace in their homes. 3) I will comfort them in all their afflictions. 4) I will be their secure refuge during life and above all in death. 5) I will bestow abundant blessings upon all their undertakings. 6) Sinners shall find in My Heart the source and the infinite ocean of mercy. 7) Tepid souls shall become fervent. 8) Fervent souls shall quickly mount to high perfection. 9) I will bless every place in which an image of My Heart shall be exposed and honored.

reparation for sins and the Five First Saturday's[24] *in honor of My Mother so that the tide of evil sweeping across the world will end in defeat. These two monthly devotions, if practiced faithfully by My followers, would alone win this battle, so great are their power in the appeasement of divine justice and the eradication of sin and evil.* Practice these devotions perpetually and you will indeed fly to Me on the wings of love as your prayer has been. You will learn to love Me in the manner in which I wish to be loved, that is, in My Humanity and Divinity joined together for eternity for the love of mankind.

"Love Me as I have loved you, giving all for love of thee. Give all to Me and I will repay you in kind beyond your imaginings. There is no greater truth than love itself, which encompasses all My commandments in loving God and one another. If you wish to follow Me, love as I have loved, sacrificing self for others and for the love of God. Peace be to you, My brothers and sisters in love. You are adopted children of God through My sacrifice on Calvary; behave as such! Amen. That is all for now. Go in peace."

---

10) I will give to priests the gift of touching the most hardened hearts. 11) Those who shall promote this devotion shall have their names written in My Heart, never to be effaced. 12) I promise thee, in the exceeding great mercy of My Heart, that its all-powerful love will grant to all those who will receive Holy Communion on nine consecutive first Fridays of the month, the grace of final repentance, not dying in My disfavor, and without receiving their sacraments, My divine Heart becoming their assured refuge at the last moment.'"—Ed.

24. The following is the message given to Sister Lucia of the Immaculate Heart (Fatima visionary), on December 10, 1925 regarding the Five First Saturdays: Christ Child: "Have compassion on the Heart of your most Holy Mother, covered with thorns, with which ungrateful men pierce it at every moment, and there is no one to make an act of reparation to remove them." Then the Holy Virgin said: "Look, my daughter, at my Heart surrounded with thorns with which ungrateful men pierce me at every moment by their blasphemies and ingratitude. You at least try to console me, and say that I promise to assist at the hour of death, with the graces necessary for salvation, all those who, on the first Saturday of five consecutive months, shall confess*, receive Holy Communion, recite five decades of the Rosary, and keep me company for fifteen minutes while meditating on the fifteen mysteries of the Rosary, with the intention of making reparation to me."

*The Confession may be made during the period of eight days, before or after the Communion—Ed.

36

Monday, March 16, 1987
Approximately 3:00 P.M.

"Queen Of All Hearts"

Vision of the Blessed Mother holding the Christ Child:

Blessed Mother: "My child, I have not forgotten you though at times it may seem that way. I never forget any of my children that are so dear to me. I do not want you to be concerned with how often you see me or my Son. We are communicating certain truths to you so that many may benefit from this wisdom.

"I hope that Father will act soon as I have instructed him. I have said enough on this subject and do not wish to reiterate this except to say that all my children should pray for a willing spirit to do the will of God.

"I am concerned with the lack of cooperation that I am receiving from many of my children who hesitate so long in doing that which I ask of them, when often it requires so little effort on their part. I want all of my priests, that is the ones dedicated to me, particularly in the M______ movement of priests, to be prompt in their response to my requests as I have explained fully in the book which you know of. I want all my children in all walks of life to now be attentive to me and my speaking to them in their everyday occurrences of life. They will know what it is that I ask of them by the circumstances which will be set forth before them. If you are called to any of my apostolates, be mindful of the duties which they entail. Do not be lax in your fulfilling of the requirements of membership, but be zealous and joyful in carrying them out, knowing full well that you are aiding in my Triumph.

"I want all my children to know that each one is precious and dear to me and has a unique role which is to be carried out by them alone and for which I have chosen them. They need not feel intimidated by the extraordinary events which may at times occur to others, even, perhaps, those who are close to them, but should rest assured in the fact that they are unique and beautiful to me and my Son in the way in which they have been created and are being formed in my Immaculate Heart for the particular mission for which they are chosen.

"Never question the ways of God. They are not your ways and are far beyond your understanding. Be content with what God has given you and do what He asks of you in your daily duty, and you will attain the perfection to which He is calling you in that state of life and in your particular situation. Never be envious or jealous of others; and remember you may not know their hidden crosses. Those who receive great gifts from God also have great crosses, and often are unable to speak of them wishing that they remain silent to increase their merit. This is a good practice and one which is pleasing to God. For if you complain of your crosses, you will lose the merit for which they are meant, diminishing it to the degree in which you are protesting. As you know, when much is given, much is expected.

"I do expect all my children to follow the requests my Son has made in calling them to the sublime vocation as members of His Mystical Body and to behave accordingly in thought, word, and action at all times. There is a certain laxness which is being tolerated even among those whom are very special to Me, in which they behave in a manner not completely in accordance with the way of perfection which I myself am now calling them to and to which my Son has called them in times gone by. Why hesitate when God calls you? Go forth in confidence in His strength and love for you. He will give you all the means necessary to accomplish what He asks of you, so you need not intellectualize about what the outcome may be before you begin an endeavor in His Name and for His glory.

"You may ask me how you know what His will is for you—by what is set forth before you to do at that time. You will know in many ways too numerous to count: by your conscience, the signs, that which falls into place, and particularly, what is set forth before you. Do not be concerned with every detail, as it is already planned for you. What you need to do is respond willingly with a generous heart.

"I will say no more for now as my Son wishes to speak to you."

Christ Child: "My Mother is the Queen of All Hearts. Honor her under this title for it will help you to carry her in your heart. She is the model, the prototype of that which I want you to be. The virtues which are manifested in her in so great abundance will likewise be found in those who are devoted to her and carry her in their hearts, in accord with the individual capacity. My desire for you now is that you all pray for these virtues so that you will be prepared to receive Me in your hearts.

"I want you to go and tend to your children now. Peace be unto your homes."

Mariamante: "Little Lord Jesus, is everything all right in regard to the concerns of which You know that I have?"

Christ Child: "Yes, but you must be patient."

37

Wednesday, March 18, 1987
5:05-6:00 P.M.

"There Are Many Reasons Why You Must Suffer"

Vision of Our Blessed Mother and the Christ Child (although only the Blessed Mother spoke):

Blessed Mother: "My Son's Passion must be your constant source of meditation throughout this Lent. I want all my children to understand this mystery through this means of prayer. God is pleased with your prayers when they come from the heart and when they are united to me in my Immaculate Heart. There are some in the Church today who would have you think that the Passion of my Son is not to be focused upon, but only the Resurrection. This cannot be, as the two cannot be separated, one leading to the other as your prayer should include. Contemplation should also include the Passion of my Divine Son and not exclusively entail the glorious aspect of Our heavenly existence. I am hoping that all my children who are called to contemplative prayer will respond to this call, which will be occurring at a rapid rate now, due to my intercession and the Triumph of my Immaculate Heart.

"I do not want you to be concerned about the persons you are thinking about. I have all these concerns in my Heart and will continue to intercede for them. They are being purified by their trials now and their resurrection, so to speak, will be most beautiful. It is when you are scoffed at and calumniated that you are brought so close to my Son. He is ever so close to the broken-hearted. He is the one you are meant to turn to in times of trial and crisis so that you can be united to His Passion and accomplish the salvific action for which it is meant. All attachments of the heart must be eventually purified if one is to attain perfection, and this is accomplished through these painful circumstances which are caused directly by my Son to bring you closer to Him. He must draw you to Himself through these painful means as it is the only way which this union can be accomplished. Do not fear it. Be prepared through prayer and penance so that when your time comes to suffer, it will be a joyful acceptance of the circumstances with this divine union in mind.

"There are many reasons why you must suffer. Do not question them. Just be willing when you are called upon. Do not fear to do that which is the will of God. It will strengthen you and make you more pleasing to Him to suffer these trials and sometimes humiliations. They bear great fruits. My hope is that my children will respond with willing spirits and generous hearts when called upon to suffer now in these times when the salvation of souls of so many are at stake. They will be with you in paradise for eternity and most grateful to you for your little sacrifices which brought about so much by the generosity of God, Who honors even the smallest attempt if it is carried out with love. Praised be the Holy Trinity now and forever! Amen.

"Go and continue doing what I have instructed you in the past. Pray for courage and I will be your strength, your courage, your fortitude, and I will prepare you for union with my Divine Son. He will dwell within you in a most glorious and beautiful fashion if you trust in Us."

38

Thursday, March 19, 1987
Feast of St. Joseph 11:35 A.M.-12:10 P.M.

"Let St. Joseph Be Their Guide And Patron"

Vision of Our Blessed Mother, then the Christ Child:

Blessed Mother: "The intensity of what is happening to you spiritually is causing your headaches. Record that you had the private conversation with me yesterday so that you will not forget to tell Father about it. He must know all that is happening to you. This is very important. It is also a safeguard for you and your protection so that no error can enter into what is occurring.

"I am pleased with your efforts in maintaining holy obedience and want you to continue in this same way. Tell Father about the Mass at ______ Catholic Church also. He needs to know what is happening to you at Mass.

"I want all my children that are receiving extraordinary gifts or experiencing extraordinary phenomena to be fully under the protection of proper spiritual direction under the auspices of

Holy Mother Church of which I am the prototype. Witness my obedience to the will of God throughout my life. Let this be your example. The Church and Her rightful authorities and representatives are whom you must answer to in regard to all facets of the spiritual life. This must be clearly understood, particularly now when there is so much confusion among the faithful as to what is happening to them in regard to spiritual happenings, that is, events that they themselves cannot fully understand or explain in the ordinary cause of events. This is not unusual, as it has occurred throughout the ages within the Church and among the people of the Old Testament. You can expect more occurrences of this nature among those who are my followers and consecrated to me. Rejoice that you live in this era, the era of mercy and love of your Mother.

"My beloved husband St. Joseph whose Feast you celebrate today is to be your example, particularly of the husbands and fathers of the families called to my apostolate of families and motherhood of which I have spoken before. Let the Holy Family guide you and be your example in all things. We will assist you in all your endeavors if they be for the glory of the Most Holy Trinity. Do all for the glory of God and in fulfillment of His will and oh what joy you will have!

"There is a need today for families to seek out time to be together and to do things together, and particularly to pray together. I want the mothers inspired to this spiritual apostolate by these writings to guide their families in this direction, as the heart of the families which they manifest.

"St. Joseph and I will intercede for you in a most powerful fashion so that the holiness of these families will be evident. Many men of today do not understand the importance of the spiritual path and are living too much in the world. *Let St. Joseph be their guide and Patron,* he who sheltered my Divine Son and myself from the world. He will help you if you pray for his assistance and will be the Patron of your families.

"The Child Jesus wishes to speak to you."

Christ Child: "My Mother is continuing to unfold her plan before you in regard to her apostolate. It is important to record all details in regard to this, as it will be the handbook for these families and inspire many to greater holiness.

"I want My Mother to be revered and honored among your families to the greatest extent. She and St. Joseph will model your families in the way in which I desire so that you will become models of Our Family when on earth. *Devotion to the Holy Family* has waned. This is unfortunate and *must be revived* in order to accomplish My plan for the world now.

"Be attentive to your Mother's voice when she speaks to you and follow her instructions carefully. I desire that all may come to Me through her Immaculate Heart. I bless you from My Heart. Now go in peace."

39

Monday, March 23, 1987
3:50-4:55 P.M.

"Holiness Is For All Of You, Not Just A Few"

Vision of the Christ Child, then the Blessed Mother and the Christ Child:

Christ Child: "You have done the correct thing in regard to this past weekend. Never fear when your intentions are good. I judge you by your intentions when doing a deed, whereas, the world simply judges by actions, never truly knowing a person's heart or mind as only his Creator can know.

"Your assumption that this message is trying to be suppressed by the evil one is likewise correct. He does not want this information to be disseminated amongst My children, having enough foreknowledge to know it will do harm to his kingdom on earth which he wishes to seize and continue to control. But alas, I have already conquered! And all his attempts are futile and in vain, for they have no true power but only assumed by his assumption of illegitimate authority over the world, which in actuality belongs to God as all things belong to God now and forever. Do not fear him, that is, the evil one, but continue to do as you have done in regard to frequent blessings from holy priests. In this fashion, your Father has helped you particularly. Frequent blessings of your home will also help in this matter.

"I am pleased with your resilience and determination to suffer on My behalf, that is, to compassionate My Holy Wounds. This is a most noble means of reparation for sin and one in which I am pleased. Do not be upset or discouraged by those who do not understand what is occurring to you; they lack the insight necessary to understand things of this nature. Do not seek their advice on any matters of faith. Seek advice only from your legitimate spiritual director.

"I wish to stress this point for all My children to understand once and for all: that I wish only priests to be involved with the discernment of spirits and things of this nature. I have given them the abilities and faculties necessary to accomplish this task, but this is not granted to all My children and should not be the practice of lay people.

"If your spiritual director tells you to do something, do it quickly and wholeheartedly as this is My expressed wish. I will not allow him to lead you astray, as this is the legitimate means of authority which I have placed over you. Likewise, if you are told not to do something, you are to obey in a wholehearted fashion, although this at times may be difficult, but will be carried out if you have a willing spirit to do My will.

"Pray for willing spirits so that when put to the test you can respond accordingly as I did with My words in the Garden of Gethsemene, 'Father, not My will but Thine be done.' This is the essence of holiness and the way you must be in all facets of your life. I have given you the perfect example that I wish all of My children to follow in this way. Holiness is for all of you not just a few, and something you must strive for through prayer and renunciation of self-will not in accord with My will.

"A most efficacious means for you to employ in this matter is the development of a higher conscience or understanding in the things of God. This will occur through much prayer and meditation and will help you in knowing My will when there is any question at hand, that is, when it may seem that there are more paths than one which you may take. The one which I have chosen for you may not always be readily apparent unless you have employed the means I stated above and maintained a recollected sense throughout your daily duty.

"I wish to live in the hearts of all men in return for their love. They will accomplish great things for Me if they follow the narrow path of holiness so often expounded upon by My great Saints, whom I have enlightened by My Holy Spirit. *The Holy Spirit, the greatest of teachers, will be your guide and light in all matters if you allow Him to penetrate your innermost being through prayer, meditation, and the contemplation of the Divine Order and majesty.*

"I am concerned with the abuses which have sprung up in regard to the movement which attributes its gifts to the Holy Spirit. Whereas, this is, of course, at times truly My Spirit at work within such individuals, there has been a stagnation on the part of many of the individuals involved in these now called charismatic prayer groups because they lack the proper direction and depth which is necessary to continue in the way of perfection—which should be a rapid spiritual growth of those united to Me, which may often occur secretly, known only to those who have the ability to discern in such matters and those themselves who are far along the spiritual path. You need not yourself be overly concerned in regard to these matters as it is the person's spiritual director who will alone be able to discern this; that is, of course, unless I choose to make these matters apparent to others as I have done in the past with My Saints who were renowned for their holiness during their lives. *They give testimony to Me by their lives and testimony to My Spirit dwelling within them in the fullness which I manifested through their heroic virtues and abilities. These should be your models, those whom you wish to emulate. They will give you insight into the ways of holiness by their lives' examples and inspire you in a singular fashion.*

"Pray to My Saints who are always ready and attentive to your supplications when they are in accord with My will. They will intercede for you so that your burdens will become slight in comparison to what they would be without such intercession. I am pleased with the revival of interest in the lives of many great Saints. This should continue so that more will benefit from their wisdom manifested by My Holy Spirit.

"Be prepared to suffer more as Lent continues. This is the royal road of suffering on which you have begun. It will continue, but I will be your strength and My Mother your inspiration. Call upon My Saints and they will hear your plea. Fortitude is a gift of the Holy Spirit and also a lesson to be learned in the natural sense. Amen. Peace be unto you and your home."

Mariamante: "Little Lord Jesus, do not leave me."

Christ Child: "Do not be frightened, My dear. All that transpires now is for your own good and will only serve to bring you closer to Me. Abandon yourself to My will and I shall see you in paradise with Me one day."

There was now a vision of the Blessed Mother:

Blessed Mother: "My Son has just told you many things that will be of great benefit to you and others when the time comes. Remember what He told you about not fearing trials or tribulations. These will only serve to bring you closer to my Son Who bore all trials and tribulations for love of mankind. He will live in you more fully when these are past, and this is the purpose of them of which you must not lose sight in the midst of them.

"Reflect upon the outcome for those who suffered, holding out to the last for love of God. The glory of the martyrs is testimony to this. Worship God and you have nothing to fear. I will be at your side in a unique fashion through these trials, and I shall be your comfort."

Mariamante: "My Mother, please strengthen me for I am weak."

Blessed Mother: "I shall."

Mariamante: "Mother, I love you."

Blessed Mother: "I know that you do, and I love you. Now go in peace."

Wednesday, March 25, 1987

40 *Feast of the Annunciation Approximately 5:00 P.M.*

Tenets Of The Apostolate Of Holy Motherhood

Vision of the Christ Child and the Blessed Mother:

Christ Child: "It is necessary for you to copy the details of the following discourse accurately for it will serve as the basis for the tenets of the apostolate of motherhood of which we have spoken in the past. *It is to be named after My Mother, the Queen of Heaven and Earth, the Mother of God, and will be called the Apostolate of Holy Motherhood in Catholic Families. This Apostolate will be approved by the Holy Father and will be promulgated amongst the families of My Church in the four corners of the earth. It will do great good and help much in stemming the tide of evil ravaging so many families today.*

"There will be three basic tenets that they, the members, must follow:

1. They[25] *must devote all their time, energy, and resources, including their very selves to the greater glory of God and the pursuit of the Divine Will in their lives;*

2. (they) must be consecrated to My Most Holy Mother under the title of 'Mother of God';

3. (they) must seek to fulfill their daily duties, that is, as mothers and wives in an exemplary manner of holiness by pursuing the contemplative life in their homes.

---

25. All members.—Mariamante.

"These three basic tenets will be expounded upon later both by Myself and My Mother so there will be much more information before this will begin.

"I do not want Father to feel rushed but there will not be a great amount of time in which to act upon this as My Mother stated earlier due to the urgency of the situation in the world today.

"My Mother wishes to speak to you."

Blessed Mother: "My dearest child, I am so pleased with what has transpired in your home in regard to the proper Catholic upbringing which your children are receiving; I wish for many mothers to do the same. You will all be receiving extraordinary graces who are members of this Apostolate, as it is divinely inspired and will be my own work."

41

Friday, March 27, 1987
4:30-5:30 P.M.

"You Must Widen Your Circle Of Prayer To Include Now The Whole Human Race"

Vision of the Christ Child and Our Blessed Mother:

Christ Child: "Pray for your brothers and sisters so steeped in sin. They are in need of your prayers. I want all My children to begin their day with prayers to My Most Holy Mother and Myself in love and reparation for sin and for the salvation of sinners. There will be times when you may forget to do this, but I do want you to say this at some point throughout the day, so that all that you do is continually being offered up for this purpose and for the greater glory of God and love of Me.

"I am disturbed by the number of My followers who do nothing to offer reparation for sin or pure love of Me, but spend most of their prayer time in petition for favors and conversion of only family members. *You must widen your circle of prayer to include now the whole human race if you wish to fulfill My will.* I am the sole judge as to when a person's heart is prepared to receive such graces of conversion, and many stand waiting to receive, yet there is no one who will make the effort to ask of this for them. Prayer is the prerequisite to spiritual favors and gifts and must be asked for by someone. You may not always know who is being helped by your prayers, but it is not necessary for you to know as all of these matters are kept in the mind of God Who will reward you in abundance for even the smallest attempt at the salvation of the souls whom He loves so tenderly.

"Ah, the love of the Most Holy Trinity is so unfathomable to your finite minds! How We long for the salvation of the souls We have created out of love. It is love which is the force that brought creation itself into existence. The desire to be sharing this love outside of the Most Holy Trinity brought mankind into existence, the creatures who are given the ability and knowledge to love even as the Father and I love with the Holy Spirit, manifesting Itself in a creative force so that We could share this joy and love and beauty with you for eternity.

"The goodness of your God is also unimaginable to you. This is something that you can only grasp at in thought for it is far beyond human comprehension. I speak here in simple language with simple terms in hopes of communicating a small aspect to those who are open to this understanding to the degree of their ability. Worship God in His goodness and love. Pray to Him in thanksgiving and joy not only in petition for wants and desires. No matter how noble they may seem, they should be only a small part of your prayer, which should mainly manifest itself in undying and fervent love for Me in the Most Holy Trinity, inflamed with zealous love fired by My Most Holy Spirit, and in praise of the Father.

"Contemplate the beauty and wisdom of the Most Holy Trinity. This you are able to do to the extent that We alone allow, in that you have been created in Our image and likeness. This should be your source of inspiration in prayer in this regard.

"My Mother is the perfect image of the unsoiled being you are all meant to be, that is, unspotted by sin or corruption of any sort. She alone has been preserved from this and given this great honor as a foreshadow of My own glory to be poured out on men in the graciousness of your God Who wished to save you from perdition.

"Sing praise to Him day and night! Rejoice in your God! Worship Him in love and reverence and awe. Be filled with My Holy Spirit so that you are able to give Him true thanks and devotion, praying one in the Spirit with Me and through Me, for all is Mine having been handed over to Me by the Father after My great sacrifice on Calvary, having proved My obedience to the last.

"I am the Way, the Truth, and the Life. Follow Me and you shall have life and have it to the fullest. Indeed, there is no life without Me and My Father for We are one in the Spirit which gives you life. You may ask Me how is it then that heathens and pagans may obtain life and come to Me in Heaven if they do not know Me on earth. This is the mystery of divine grace which is applied to each according to his or her ability to receive. Each soul is given the moment or hour to accept and understand before death[26] and, thereby, attain what has been planned for them even before their individual creation. That is how they may attain salvation. Whereas, those who know of Me but willingly reject Me are the ones who are in need of repentance so that they may attain to their immortal home.

"Alas, I have prepared a banquet for you. Taste and see the goodness of the Lord Who loves you so, having gone before you with such sufferings on your behalf and to attain your salvation. Do not let Me down; do not forsake that which is so holy for mere things of the world which will waste away in due time. Store up your treasures in Heaven where I will reward you with joy and peace beyond your understanding now.

"I am pleased with the initiative which Father has taken and I am about to lift his burden in a certain regard which I am not making known to you. He will find life easier for the time being and will receive a period of peace.

"I am pleased with the accomplishments of many of My children, especially those consecrated to My Most Holy Mother, in their prayers and works towards her Triumph and their own personal prayer lives. Remember by continuing in your present efforts you are being strengthened in perseverance and will eventually obtain all you hoped for and even more. As you know, God will never be outdone in generosity. Now go in peace."

Blessed Mother: "My Son has said all that you need to know for today. Now go in peace."

There was a brief private exchange at the end, telling each other we loved one another.

26. I took this to refer to baptism of desire as understood by the Church.—Mariamante.

42

Tuesday, March 31, 1987
3:10 P.M.

"A New Work Of The Lord"

Vision of Our Blessed Mother and the Christ Child:

Blessed Mother: "This Lent has been an ordeal for you, but it is not yet over, and you must be secure in Our love for you and remain steadfast in your love for Us, as this is meant to be a trial of the will similar to which We spoke of before. The suppression will eventually end, and your husband will again have peace, but he must go to Confession because of his sins. They are being compounded daily and he must ask for forgiveness. Pray for him in this way that he will be cleansed of his sins and return to the grace and peace of Our Lord Jesus Christ.

"I am unable to convey to you the importance of these trials for they are doing a tremendous service to your soul by strengthening your endurance, gaining steadfastness, and learning fortitude in the midst of tribulation. My Son Who suffered in the most complete sense of the word must always be your source of inspiration during these trials so that you will not grow fainthearted but remain steadfast and resolute in your service of God by His supreme example of the Passion. My child, all your trials are so slight in comparison to His. Always remember this and you will have the proper perspective in order to gain from your own. He has in a sense already won them for you by His own trials but you must still submit your own willing spirit to the test. It is a requirement of those who would gain Heaven.

"As sinners you are all in need of constant help and support of the sacraments. These sanctifying graces you receive through them will be all you need to triumph over any trial and continue to transform you into images and likenesses of my Divine Son. He has instituted the sacraments for this purpose to help you to attain Heaven, and you must always turn to them for your strength, particularly, of course, the Sacrament of Penance and Holy Eucharist.

"I know that it has become very difficult for you to receive Holy Communion of late[27] but this also is part of your trial

27. Because I was unable to get to daily Mass for a time and could Communicate only on Sundays and occasionally during the week.—Mariamante.

so you must not lose heart. Take courage and continue to make frequent spiritual communions which will strengthen you.

"Those who wish to be in service of the Lord can always expect these sorts of occurrences for it is the path to Him. My Child wishes to speak to you."

Christ Child: "Patient endurance is beginning to be manifested in you because of these trials, so that you can be more like Me. I am pouring forth My Spirit upon you and others who are enduring similar trials, often unbeknownst to those receiving such in abundance.

"Be prepared for extraordinary circumstances to begin to occur to you and others who have likewise been chosen to fulfill My will in an extraordinary fashion. They will be pleased and surprised to know there are more than one of you who is receiving similar graces to accomplish My will.

"My Mother's plan to accomplish the Triumph of her Immaculate Heart has been underway now for sometime and continues to gain momentum as more souls consecrated to her are called forth to begin their particular mission for which they are picked. This is why it is of the utmost importance that you do all that is asked of you down to the letter so as not to leave any part of her plan not accomplished through your own negligence.

"It is sometimes necessary to step out in faith before something can be accomplished. This is indeed the case in this matter.

"I want Father to devote more time to this project and to begin to set aside time for this task to be accomplished as it will be necessary. There are many who will be helped by all of this, which is why My Mother and I have given this information to you: for the benefit of others, not only yourselves.

The Apostolate We wished to begin has been explained and announced on the Feast of the Annunciation, which is fitting as it will be the Mother of God to whom the members are consecrated, and will aid them in treating their children and families with the proper reverence which is being requested through this Apostolate. This *reverence for the person of Christ in all persons, and particularly nowadays children,* is the reason for this. They should strive to fulfill their daily tasks in accord with the spirit in which she carried out her tasks while on earth. This will be a constant source of contemplation throughout their day, so that all that they do will be in accord with the will of God. I am pleased with the attempts you have made thus far in fulfilling this request. Continue to do the same.

"Even as the Angel Gabriel announced to My Mother the inception of My Incarnation, so We have announced to you the beginning of a new work of the Lord on the same day. This work will be in accord with the yearnings of My Heart in the salvation of many sinners and should not be delayed in its inception. There is nothing to fear in that this will be purely a work of joy and love for those involved because I will make it so for them.

"Praise the Holy Trinity! Now go in peace even as I bless you."

43

Thursday, April 2, 1987
12:30 P.M.

"Carrying The Cross"

Vision of the Christ Child:

Christ Child: "There are many suffering from such woes which you have. This is due to the wickedness of the world. As you know, the world did not recognize Me nor will it recognize My followers. You must be in the world but not of it. This you are accomplishing well and must continue to do so. I am pleased with the sufferings which you are enduring on My behalf. These are the greatest sort of suffering because they are for the love of God that you are being persecuted. It has always been so throughout the ages. Do not forget this and tell Father the same. My children must take heart in remembering the lives of My Saints who endured all manner of trials for the love of Me and My most Holy Church. Indeed, it must be this way in order for you to truly follow in My footsteps. Carrying the cross is meant to be difficult in order for it to bear much fruit. The degree of your suffering will indicate the degree of the sanctity you are attaining through My grace. I wish to live fully within My children and this is how it will be accomplished, this metanoia of which you have heard.

"Welcome Me into your heart as the Prince of Peace in the midst of all tribulations and I shall give you the peace necessary to endure them and to triumph over all evil in your life. You will be images of Me living in the world today. You must not neglect to pray for those who are persecuting you, for it is by your prayers and sufferings that their salvation is wrought.

"I have come to save sinners not the just. The just are already members of My Father's house as the prodigal son's brother who had the advantages of never leaving the father's house. But all Heaven rejoices at the repentance of one sinner. I shall continue later. Tend to the children for now."

Later the same day, while in prayer
Thursday, April 2, 1987 5:40 P.M.

Vision of the Christ Child:

Christ Child: "I am pleased with your efforts, but you must find a more suitable time.[28] Now go be with your children."[29]

44

Monday, April 6, 1987
4:55 P.M.

"My Mother Has Been Most Gracious"

Vision of the Christ Child:

Christ Child: "My Mother has been most gracious to the sons of men."

The children interrupted during which time the baby woke up, so remembering what He had said in the vision in the previous week, about going to be with the children, I did not go back to pray.

45

Thursday, April 9, 1987
7:10-7:45 P.M.

"The Gate By Which You Enter Heaven"

Vision of the Blessed Mother:

Blessed Mother: "It is not important as to where the visions take place. What is important is the message We are giving to you. The

28. For prayer.—Mariamante.
29. I think He said this because two of the children were up and it was dinner time. I had returned to pray though, because earlier in the day He had said, "I shall continue later." This I took to mean later that day. But apparently His wish was for me to eat dinner with the children. I did as He instructed.—Mariamante.

light which you see is an indication that the event occurring is of the supernatural origin. We can, of course, communicate with you by any means, but have chosen this one, as it best suits your station in life and is not obstructive to your daily duties as a mother and wife.

"The trance by which you are effected is due to the communication process and the visions which produce this effect. If Father wishes to know more about these occurrences he should refer to that which has already been written on them and witness this occurring to you. The Dialogue of St. Catherine of Siena will indeed be helpful to him as you suspected, as this is a similar form of communication, although hers was of a more sublime nature.

"It is indeed necessary for Father to read these papers as he receives them in order for him to be able to understand what is unfolding before him. The need for the Apostolate We have mentioned is well established.

"Rest in my Immaculate Heart and do not worry about the fulfillment of my plan as I will fulfill it myself through you my children as the instruments.

"You are nearing the end of your Lenten trial. You can be thankful that you have endured it well. Praise the Sacred Heart of Jesus, my Divine Son. His Heart is the abyss of mercy for all sinners. *The wound in His Heart is the gate by which you enter Heaven* in that it was pierced by and for sinners like yourself. He is Mercy Incarnate as He is Love Incarnate. His Eucharistic Heart is the same as His Sacred Heart. They are inseparable in nature.

"Do not fear. It is Us. See the wound in His Heart and the light around Our Hearts. This is emphasized to draw your attention to the true meaning of love: He was pierced for your iniquities. Now keep your promise and do what you are told."

Friday, April 10, 1987
3:50 P.M.

46

"Worship Me In Spirit And In Truth"

Vision of the Christ Child:

Christ Child: "There is no time to be wasted now. You must act quickly as We instructed you. I am going to help you to know what I want you to say and when to say it. This prompting of the Holy Spirit will be in accord with what I promised My disciples when instructing them not to fear when put to the test as I would give them the Holy Spirit to be speaking through them and would give them the words to say. This prompting of the Holy Spirit will enable you and others to whom I grant it the ability to counter questions accurately when being scrutinized so that it will be apparent that what is occurring here is of Me and divine origin rather than yourself.

"I know that it will not always be easy for you to endure what is about to occur to you but it must be this way for now. My Mother will continue to give you Her powerful protection in the midst of all situations and you will never be abandoned by Me for I love you so and have picked you from the beginning of time for this which is about to occur to you."

Mariamante: "Lord, I dare not ask what it is. I just trust in Thee."

Christ Child: "Do not fear, My child, for even in your darkest moments there will be light, the light which is I Myself, the light of the world and the light of your heart. Worship Me in spirit and in truth from the depths of your heart and I will live in you to the fullest as I have done before in My Saints. I love you. Now go in peace."

Mariamante: "Little Lord Jesus, please help my husband to go to Confession."

Christ Child: "I will, this Holy Week."[30]

---

30. This promise did come true. In fact, it happened in a manner that was most unusual and stunning for it was at a time when it appeared as impossible to be accomplished. At the same time, the Pilgrim Virgin of Fatima statue was in our home. It often exudes sweet fragrances, such as roses, flowers, perfume, and incense while at our house. It did so the day this promise was fulfilled.—Mariamante.

47

Monday, April 13, 1987
Monday of Holy Week 6:15 P.M.

"I Am Your Mother And I Shall Protect You"

Vision of the Blessed Mother:

Blessed Mother: "Do not fear, my child. I am with you. I shall be your way to the Son and through Him to the Father. There are many things that you do not yet understand in regards to the mission to which We have entrusted you. You must be completely submissive to the will of God in all things. The number of souls who respond to my warnings will make the difference.

"Do not be concerned with human respect. It is worthless and can be detrimental. I want you to continue in what you have been doing while Father is gone.

"I do not want you to be discouraged with what may seem to be defeats, but remain steadfast in your faith and you shall triumph over all that may now seem impossible. I am your Mother and I shall protect you. You have nothing to fear, even the wrath of those closest to you. This is unavoidable and part of the spiritual path for those who would love me and my Divine Son. Consider it your cross. All must suffer the scorn of the world in order to be made more like my Son. I too grieve over your sufferings and hold them all within my heart. Do not forget that I too know what it is to suffer in fulfilling the will of the Lord. This is the way it must be. But rejoice, be glad that you have been chosen to be counted among those whom He calls blessed. You will rejoice with Us in Heaven someday for your steadfastness during persecution.

"Remember what I have told you in the past and continue to do your work for the Lord. I will never leave you. Go now in peace."

Mariamante: "My Mother, strengthen me."

Blessed Mother: "I will."

Mariamante: "And make me into a likeness of Jesus."

Blessed Mother: "I will."

48

Thursday, April 16, 1987
Holy Thursday 5:00-5:30 P.M.

"You Must Soften Your Hearts"

Visions (one following the other) of the Blessed Mother with a sorrowful expression and a drawn appearance and tears; Our Blessed Mother with Her Immaculate Heart exposed; and Our Lord as an adult with His Sacred Heart exposed:

Blessed Mother: "You are becoming too distant from me and my Son; this is my message to the world on this Holy Thursday. Turn back and repent before it is too late. There is too much sin and it is offending God too much. It cannot go on much longer. You have been warned time and time again, yet most fail to hear my pleadings and those that do often do not put them into practice.

"You must soften your hearts. This is your answer. Harden not your hearts if today you hear His voice. He has given all for you and you give Him so little in return. Why is this? And how can it be that you are so ungrateful to a God Who loves you so, having manifested His love so completely and perfectly in His sublime Passion and Resurrection. I have no more to say. My Son wishes to speak to you now. I have said everything there is to say at Fatima and elsewhere in my apparitions. Now listen to my Son."

Jesus: "My beloved child, behold My Heart wounded for your sins. It gushes forth with a ceaseless river of grace for My children so weakened in sin. They do not understand how their sins hurt Me in a personal way. *I want you to make reparation to the Wound in My Heart, the manifestation of My brokenness for the sins of mankind.* My Heart is broken by their sins. Make reparation to Me for this outrage and console your God.

"I am pleased thus far with your attempts, but I am about to ask much more of you. My Mother will be your guide throughout this difficult time for you, but you must not hesitate in fulfilling the will of God. I have chosen many to aid Me in this fashion and you will be one of them."

Mariamante: "I do not hesitate, Lord, fiat. Whatever Thy will is, be it done unto me, only grant me the strength to endure so as never to offend Thee."

Jesus: "My child, you do not as yet understand many things, but you will soon know more."

Mariamante: "I only wish to do Your will, Lord God."

Jesus: "Yes, I know. Now go in peace."

49

Friday, April 17, 1987
Good Friday 1:10-1:45 P.M.

"Contemplate My Passion"

Vision of Mother of Sorrows, then Our Lord with His Sacred Heart exposed:

Blessed Mother: "These visions will end for a time; and you will fall into disregard among many. There will be times when you yourself will have great doubts about what is happening to you. This will be the dark night for you, the period of cleansing and sanctification which will be necessary for my Divine Son to live more fully in you. When it is past, you will enter a glorious period indeed. I will be with you through it all. Have faith and persevere in all that you have been doing for the Lord. You will be reviled by many for a time, even those closest to you, but do not fear, for your help is in the name of the Lord Who will deliver you from all tribulation when the time is at hand.

"My Son wishes to speak to you."

Jesus: "My child, do not forget My Passion. Ponder it as you have today, the Passion, your redemption. The world does not understand the Passion because the depth of its meaning escapes those that are not of Me. They are unable to grasp its meaning because it is beyond mere human understanding. The wisdom of God is beyond human thought or understanding. This is why I have given you My Holy Spirit that you may understand that which is of God.

"Praise the Holy Trinity. *Contemplate My Passion* and remember My love for you; a love such as this no man has but I. *I have laid down My life for the salvation of the world and the world knows Me not.* Console your God, make reparation for sin in all that you do and tell others the same. *Return love for love, as this is the most fitting form of reparation; none other surpasses it.* In it I am well pleased.

"Be kind to one another and follow My example in all things. Invite Me into your hearts so that I may accomplish the will of the Father for each one of you as I have accomplished it on My own behalf.

"Be not afraid. Your God loves you. I shall bless you now and I want you to go to the tabernacle. *Worship the Blessed Sacrament. It is My Sacred Heart wounded for mankind.*"

50

Tuesday, April 28, 1987
6:05-6:35 P.M.

"The Way Of Perfection"

Vision of the Christ Child:

Christ Child: "Trust in Me and write what I tell you. The wickedness of the world at this time is unsurpassed. Witness the victimization of small children and the unborn. Never before has this been done on such a wide scale as it is today. This offends My Heavenly Father in a most severe fashion. He is prepared to cleanse the world of its sin, but the hand of justice is held back by those who are making reparation for sin to Myself and My Mother. This is why I want you to spend your time making acts of reparation throughout your day and accepting all that God gives you in a patient manner.

"Live prayer-filled existences without complaint and always in union with Me and My Sacred Heart and My Mother's Immaculate Heart. We are eager to help all who call upon Us with sincerity and wish to amend their lives. Pray for those who do not yet know Me. They will receive their enlightenment in due time, an eternal rose in bloom for eternity for those who have helped convert that soul through prayer and sacrifice.

"I am calling many souls to respond to My boundless love, but so many are in such a sad state, so filled with sin and the world. If those who know and serve Me will make heroic efforts now, many of these will be converted due to the extraordinary era of mercy in which you are living.

"I am asking now for the help of My followers, particularly, those devoted to My most Holy Mother, to fight this battle with her for the souls so in peril. The evil one is arrogant in his presumption of having won many souls. However, Heaven's plan is infinitely more powerful and grand and will encompass many who would otherwise perish at the hands of the enemy who is now so active. My Mother's cause is what you must be dedicated to fulfilling. She will continue to instruct you in the precise manner in which this will be accomplished.

"I do not want you to be concerned with how these predictions will be fulfilled. Only trust is necessary, and, as you know from past experience, I shall never give you more than you can bear. This is part of My merciful plan for all souls, that they be purified while on this earth so they can join Me in Heaven upon their death. I do not wish to see them linger in Purgatory, but desire for them to come immediately to Me upon their death. This is the way of perfection upon this earth of which you have heard. Practice it well, so that you may be one who is united to Me on earth and upon your death. I am speaking to many when I speak to you. These are basic truths which I wish to make known to those who would otherwise not come in contact with them or would not be able to understand them in more sublime terms.

"You have served Me well thus far. Continue to do so and encourage others to do the same. This is the time for forgiveness and mutual effort for the salvation of souls. Do not let anything deter you from this mission to which you have been entrusted by My Mother.

"Continue to follow Father's guidance which is divinely inspired in regards to your soul.

"I will bless you now. Continue to seek the blessings of holy priests. This will aid you in your quest for holiness and offer protection to your soul."

Mariamante: "Little Lord Jesus, I love You. Please grant that I may do all according to Your holy will and the design of Your most Holy Mother."

Christ Child: "I shall. Go now in peace and tend to your duties with love."

51

Saturday, May 2, 1987
During the day

"Adore The Blessed Sacrament"

A vision of Our Blessed Mother and Our Lord as an adult at ______ Catholic Church while kneeling in front of the May Crowning Statue of Our Blessed Mother:

Blessed Mother: "Adore the Blessed Sacrament. . ."[31]

52

Sometime between May 2 and May 12, 1987 (date unrecorded)
4:30-4:55 P.M.

"The Sacraments Are Essential To The Salvation Of All Mankind"

Vision of the Christ Child:

Christ Child: "Obedience is your protection. Continue in this regard. You are only separated by miles from your Father. This is no distance at all in the spiritual realm. Continue to pray for him for holiness and to do God's will. He needs your prayers also as do all My children living in this iniquitous era. My Mother is devoted to her priest sons and wishes their devotion in return. This you can aid by your prayers.

"I want all My priests to be devoted to My Mother. If all could only begin to understand the immensity of My love for My Mother and wish to imitate it in their own small fashion, I will be pleased with their attempts and reward them with abundant graces and blessings. I am concerned with the number who have lost sight of the importance of this aspect of the faith and continue as if it is not important.

"Cultivate devotion to My Mother and especially to her Immaculate Heart by your prayers and through this Apostolate. Part of your

---

31. Our Blessed Mother also said something to the effect of: "You have done well so far in your attempts. Adore the Blessed Sacrament." Although now I cannot remember all verbatim, as this is now Monday, May 4, on which I am recording this. I went immediately to the tabernacle after this vision and did as she said. I had also been praying before the tabernacle before I went to the statue where I had the vision.—Mariamante.

prayer vocation should be in the pursuit of prayers for priests as they are, of course, essential to the spreading of My kingdom on earth and the continuance of the faith. Without the sacraments all would be lost.

"The sacraments are essential to the salvation of all mankind and these come to you through My priests. Pray for them always for holiness and spiritual perfection, particularly now for a detachment from worldly things.

"The world continues to erode away at the base of the faith, My Church. It is now necessary to set up a bulwark to stop this erosion which is holiness itself. Pray for holiness among My priests and yourselves, the laity, and you will see a difference in the world. You must be the instruments of My holiness on earth as the world knows Me not.

"I wish to reveal more of My plan to you soon through My Mother. Now go in peace as I bless you from My Heart."

Mariamante: "Lord, have mercy on me and make my heart like unto Thine."

Christ Child: "I will."

53

Tuesday, May 12, 1987
2:30-2:53 P.M.

"My Mercy Is Boundless"

Vision of the Christ Child:

Christ Child: "You have many fears which you must renounce. You are learning to see with the eyes of your soul. If you are to understand things of the spirit this is necessary, that you see all in this manner, that is, in the spiritual sense as with the eyes of your soul. This is both literal and figurative at times.

"As We have told you before, We do not want you to be concerned with the fulfillment of these prophecies, as it will be taken care of and is out of your hands as to how they are to be accomplished. Your mission is to pray that God's will be done upon the earth at this time. My Mother is your advocate and the one who will lead you to sanctity if you comply with Our requests. I know that you are concerned with the situation in regards to. . . I want you to be at peace about this situation, not in constant turmoil. However, this period has been used as part of your own purification as was foretold to you earlier.

"But the time has now come for you to be at peace about it. My Mother will see to this on your behalf tomorrow as this is her special day and one in which she is to be venerated in a particular fashion of love, and fortitude in which one seeks only to do the will of God as she requested at Fatima in years gone by.

"My Mother continues to protect and intercede for you. For this you can be most grateful and thankful to her. For as My mercy is boundless so is her intercession which remains constant for you and others who are so devoted to her with love.

"I do not want you to neglect your duties so go and tend to the child. We will continue later."

I asked for His blessing at the end and waited for it. My son had come home from school when He said the last few words.

54

Tuesday, May 19, 1987
11:10 A.M.

"Love My Son Jesus"

Vision of Our Blessed Mother and the Christ Child:

Blessed Mother: "Go and copy what has already been given to you in vision to be prepared for Father's return. We, my Son and I, wish for you to prepare in prayer before the Feast of Pentecost with a special novena to the Holy Spirit which will be given to you. Repeat this prayer for nine days before and after the feast, first in petition, then in thanksgiving:

'Come Holy Spirit, enlighten my heart to see the things which are of God;
Come Holy Spirit into my mind that I may know the things that are of God;
Come Holy Spirit into my soul that I may belong only to God.
Sanctify all that I think, say, and do that all will be for the Glory of God. Amen.'

"You are concerned that the meeting with Father ______ was not as you expected. This is because it was not yet time. When you meet on Pentecost it will be different and as I foretold. The gift you received yesterday of being able to go was due to the intercession of St. Anthony as you had prayed to him in earnest. He is suppliant to your prayers and a great advocate for many in Heaven. Continue to enlist his aid as he is one of your special patrons, a spiritual father to you and a Franciscan brother.

"Do not neglect the details of your daily duty in your zealousness for souls to love God, as this is part of the very way in which you will draw them closer to God. By this means and through prayer many are being called to intercede for others and make recompense for sinners despite their own imperfections. This is due to God's mercy. Many sinners are now not aware of God's love and have no knowledge of Him. You are being called to pray for them and to make atonement for their sins.

"Love my Son Jesus. This is my mandate to you. Love Him with the intensity of all your heart and ask that the Holy Spirit and myself be always present in your heart and soul that We may form Jesus Christ within you. This will be the foreshadowing of my Triumph when complete. I speak to many when I speak to you.

"Remember my words and do what you are told. Now go in peace and love for my beloved Son Jesus."

55

Sunday, May 24, 1987
11:55 A.M.

"Age Of The Two Hearts"

Vision of Our Lord with His Sacred Heart exposed:

Jesus: *"The Sacred and Immaculate Hearts are to be the constant source of your inspiration and the focus of your prayer. This is the age of the Two Hearts and the way in which We wish to be venerated and honored.* The depth of this devotion escapes many who are looking to relate to their God in what they blindly perceive to be some modern form, which is none other than a lessening of the degree of holiness of which men are to aspire. They seek to relate in only human terms when My command to them is to be perfect even as My Heavenly Father is perfect. This requires a form of supernatural love which is made available to you in abundance through the devotion to the Two Hearts. It is through this means that you are able to love in a similar fashion in which My Mother and I love and glorify the Father.

"Your humanity is exalted by this means, which then enables you to be more divine than human in your love. Love, the queen of all virtues, an inflamed love, fired by My Holy Spirit, poured out upon you through these powerful devotions to the Two Hearts. Beg the Holy Spirit to come into your hearts through this means and you will experience a quickening in the degree of sanctity to which you are attaining.

"My Mother's Heart is your heavenly garden of perfumed spices, the flower which adorns the Most Holy Trinity with love so abundant. My Heart is the source of this love for her and for you which is refused to none who request it with childlike confidence in their Redeemer Who loves them in an infinite fashion.

"As the Holy Spirit unites the Father and I in love beyond human comprehension, so the love of My Most Holy Mother and I is similar, in a lesser degree but yet infinite also in nature. This is due to My twofold nature of God and man. I call all to love in a similar fashion according to the degree of their ability as they are created. Although none can love to the perfection of My Heavenly Mother, they are nevertheless called to imitate this love in their own unique fashion, thereby giving glory to God in a unique and precious way similar to the love of little children in its uniqueness.

"I wish to pour forth My Spirit upon mankind and to save all from destruction and the forces of evil so prevalent in the world today. None except the most spiritually blind can deny the rampant evils of this age. Yet I yearn for these souls with a tender and solicitous love. Help Me to win them back. Help them to love Me by your prayers for the glory of the Father in Heaven. They are precious to Me despite their sins. I call them to Me. Come, My little ones, I am your Shepherd, the Shepherd of your souls. Come follow Me to your heavenly home where you will find rest and peace and joy.

"See, I have prepared a banquet for you and I wish for you to rest at My table in My Father's house. There We will live together forever in joy and peace. Amen.

"Praise the Holy Trinity! Worship Me in the Blessed Sacrament. Adore My Sacred Heart. Venerate My Mother with tender devotion in a childlike fashion.

"Go in peace."

56

Monday, May 25, 1987
6:15 P.M.

"Intercession Of The Saints"

Vision of Our Lord with His Sacred Heart exposed, His face looked very beautiful:

Jesus: "St. Anthony is interceding for you. Continue to invoke his aid. He and your Seraphic Father Francis are eager to help their children on earth. This is why he keeps coming into your path. They understand your weakness and are able to supply what you are lacking in faith in your prayers.

"This is the purpose of the intercession of the Saints, that is, to supply what you are lacking so as to make your prayers and works more pleasing to God Who is worthy of only the most perfect of intentions.

"My Mother's intercession remains a constant for you but you must continue to invoke her aid in all your endeavors so they will be made more perfect by her intercession. She remains the supreme example of all intercessory power of the Saints. In her I am well pleased. Therefore, in those who are united to her I am also pleased.

"Do not be overly concerned with the externals of the spiritual life but rather with what is internal, that is, the will and the intent of all thoughts, words, and actions.

"Retain a recollected sense at all times and you shall have peace. The busyness of the world is not conducive to deep prayer, which is why you must maintain a distance from the world even when in it.

"You are concerned with your unworthiness, and this is something which cannot be helped as it is a divine truth that all are unworthy of the favors which God grants to His children, yet He freely wishes to grant them, thereby, making you in a sense worthy of His own volition rather than by anything you yourself can or could do to merit this grace.

"Now go in peace and joy and do not be anxious."

Mariamante: "Lord, grant that I may do all for Thee and for Thy glory."

Jesus: "I shall, but you must be kind to all who come across your path. This is a necessity. Now go in peace."

57

Thursday, May 28, 1987
Feast of the Ascension

"Adoring His Sacred Countenance"

A vision of Our Lord. His Sacred Face was different than I had ever seen before, although it is difficult to put into words. There was a private conversation, after which He said I should study His Face closely, as it would be impressed upon my heart as I had requested, and this would be for the purpose of adoring His Sacred Countenance in reparation for the sins of outrages and blasphemies. At this point, I fell into a rapture-like state lasting for quite some time, after which I awoke feeling very peaceful with a gentle quality that I cannot fully describe.

58

Sunday, May 31, 1987
11:30 A.M.

"Adore My Sacred Heart"

Vision of Our Lord with His Sacred Heart exposed:

Jesus: "I am the Way, the Resurrection and the Life. He who comes to Me will never thirst. The hour has come for you to drink from the living waters, the water of life which is grace, the grace of My life poured out in abundance upon all who call upon Me in their distress.

"Come to Me, all who are thirsty and I will give you rest. Come and drink of the living waters where you will find your refreshment, the peace from your toils and labors of life. I know your needs for it is I Who have created you. I know your worries and the problems of life in this world. I ask you to trust Me and to transcend it all by My grace.

"Behold the Heart which has loved mankind so much and been loved so little in return. Love Me as you should and I will live in you. Adore My Sacred Heart bruised for your iniquities. Make recompense for your sins by this devotion and have life in the fullest through it.

"My Mother's heart will be your repose, the garden from which you adore your Heavenly Savior Who also rested there in life. My Heart will free you from your troubles if you will abandon yourself to Me in this devotion.

''Oh, love so abundant in the Heart of My Mother! Imitate this love of hers for Me. Smell the perfume, the fragrance of love.

''The fire which burns in My Heart, the furnace of charity, is too deep for you alone; call upon My Mother to aid you in this quest.''

59

Monday, June 1, 1987
4:45 P.M.

''Come To Me, Children Of My Mother''

Vision of Our Lord with His Sacred Heart exposed:

Jesus: ''The abyss of charity and virtue which is My Heart is yours for the asking. I wish to give My Heart to all who call upon Me in faith and love. I am in need of those to love Me in reparation for the sins of the world. Do not hesitate in your call. Come to Me now with willing hearts and spirits inflamed by My Holy Spirit with a supernatural love in atonement for sins.

''Come to Me, children of My Mother, spouses of Mine picked from the beginning of time and nurtured in the womb of My Mother, made pure by her virtues, for Me. Learn from her. Imitate her virtues. Follow her example if you wish to please Me.

''I am meek and humble of heart. Give Me your humility. I am meek; give Me your meekness. I am love incarnate; give Me your love. Hope in Me that you will be made worthy by the remission of your sins and the heroic virtue of My Mother to be imitated by all. Be living furnaces of charity for God and one another. Be forgiving and kind.

''Come now to Me and I will give you rest. Amen I say to you, He who passes to Heaven will do so through My Heart. Amen. Now go in peace.''

Mariamante: ''Lord, please set my heart on fire for Thee that I may love You as I should with all the powers of my being.''

Jesus: ''I will, even as you ask of it.''

After He said this I was caught up in a rapture so deep it lasted quite some time, perhaps a half hour, in which time I at times prayed in a poetic fashion composing prayers and poems of love to Our Lord and Our Blessed Mother. Some of them are as follows which I wrote down after I came out of this state:

Mariamante: Oh Mother, adorn my heart with thy love.
Adorn my mind with thy faith.
Adorn my soul with thy purity and virtues in fullness,
That I may be made worthy to be a spouse of Jesus Christ, the King of Kings. Amen.

Make my heart a garden in which He may rest and repose His Sacred Head.

Oh Love Divine! Come dwell within me.
Make Thy abode within my heart!

My Mother's Heart is a rose.
In parting the petals, I find My Jesus there,
beautiful to behold,
splendid in white,
shining in radiance.

My God, I love Thee, let me sing Thy praises forever!
Thou art all beautiful and good,
sweetness and light,
joy and peace. Amen.

My Mother will make up for in what I am lacking. She will make me pleasing to Christ.

60

Thursday, June 4, 1987
3:00 P.M.

"Do Not Be Frightened Of Trials"

Vision of Our Lord, then Our Blessed Mother:

Jesus: "It will become increasingly difficult for you to continue to escape unnoticed. This will be part of your cross as it has been for many before you. Although the persons who will be speaking about you are to be prayed for, do not let them have any great effect on you as it is not important what is said of you by those of ill will. There will be many times at which you will wish to run and flee from the sight of others, but do not fear as I will be with you and you will have My protection along with My Mother's. She will help to soften the hearts of those who will be speaking of you unfavorably.

"The nature of these visions will not be revealed to others, but you will suffer in regards to other spiritual happenings which others will not understand except Father and those who are now fulfilling My will amongst your associates.

"Do not be overly concerned about all of this, as it is part of the spiritual path for all those attaining perfection. Many of My Saints suffered greatly for their piety at the hands of the impious. But you will be spared much as We wish to protect your family from trials beyond their endurance at this time. My Mother will protect you; call upon her."

Blessed Mother: "My Son has spoken to you of trials and I wish to speak to you of love, with tender love of a mother for her children. Do not be frightened of trials, rather accept them joyfully as your true path to the Lord. I will provide for you in every detail so you will receive a mother's protection.

"Go now and do not be afraid of what will come to pass as it is necessary. Peace be with you, my child. Now go in peace."

Mariamante: "My Mother, please protect me and provide for all my necessities that I may do the will of the Lord."

Blessed Mother: "I will."

61

Friday, June 5, 1987
First Friday 3:35 P.M.

"Purgatory"

Vision of Our Lord with His Sacred Heart exposed:

Jesus: "The living waters of grace are available to you through the sacraments. Avail yourselves of them. By this means you will be kept free and spotless of sins. The graces of the confessional will sustain you in the turmoil of your own spiritual life and strengthen you in virtue.

"My Father's plan for each one of you is that your sins be forgiven while on earth. However, for those many souls who do not avail themselves of this means, He has mercifully created a place of atonement after death. There are many souls who long to be released from Purgatory. Pray for them. These holy souls can also aid you in your journey if you call upon them. They can pray for you."

62

Sunday, June 7, 1987
Pentecost Sunday, Beginning of the Marian Year

Prophecy Fulfilled

While at ______ Catholic Shrine, I was given two silent visions. A prophecy which was given to me by the Blessed Mother earlier in these messages regarding what would occur on Pentecost, was fulfilled.

63

Tuesday, June 9, 1987
8:45 A.M.

"Be Not Afraid To Be Called Forth"

Vision of the Christ Child:

Christ Child: "Do not fear; all is not lost, but Father must act quickly if he does not wish to lessen the effect that this Apostolate will have in the world. As We have said before, a quick and generous response from the heart when called forth by the will of God is what is necessary if the evils of your time are to be combated. If the good are lax in their response to God's call, they will lessen the effect of the graces which are being poured forth upon the earth at the intercession of My Most Holy Mother and due to My mercy.

"Be not afraid to be called forth. Trust in Me and My Mother that you may not be led astray. We wish to lead you only to extraordinary holiness; indeed, this is the case for all who would answer My call perfectly and fulfill the will of My Father perfectly for them on earth.

"But there are so few who respond in this fashion, even when called by extraordinary graces. They turn away from the call I give them and settle for less than the way of perfection.

"How sad this makes Me. Have I not given you everything? Why must you hesitate when I ask you to give to Me in return what you have received by My grace and mercy alone? I say again, do not squander your graces, do not squander what I have given to you lest you be as the man with the buried talents when the master returns to make an accounting and finds no increase with what he the servant was entrusted with.

"My Mother and I have entrusted you both with a mission

that is beyond your comprehension at this point. You must trust in God so that it will be fulfilled.

"Do not be troubled too much by what is going on around you. There is great confusion now and much talk. Be silent to combat the excessive talk. Be good to combat the evil. Be holy to combat the unholiness. Fear nothing but sin.

"Follow what you are told and continue in faithfulness to the will of God. If you have concerns, speak to your Father about them without fear so that he too may be enlightened as to the negative forces which surround him.

"Respond generously to My call. We have come to ask for your willing spirits that My Mother's Triumph may occur on the face of the earth. You are fortunate to be called as such; be thankful! Now go in peace."

Mariamante: "Little Lord Jesus, please give us willing spirits..."

Christ Child: "You must be truthfully willing to do the will of God in all things even if it involves the extraordinary. This is particularly the case with Father. And you need to be more receptive to the will of God in your own life.

"Now go in peace even as I bless you."

64

Wednesday, June 10, 1987
2:20-2:50 P.M.

"The Era Of My Mercy Has Come"

Vision of Our Lord and Our Blessed Mother with Their Sacred and Immaculate Hearts exposed:

Jesus: "The Triumph of My Mother's Immaculate Heart has already begun. Rejoice and be glad that you are part of it. The reign of My Sacred Heart is the fulfillment of the promises of Fatima, that is, the reign of peace which was foretold. This era of peace which will encompass the world will be the result of the Triumph of the Immaculate Heart of Mary, My Mother. The deplorable conditions in which the world now finds itself will be transformed into the likeness of My Father's kingdom for a time and there will be peace.

"I say again, rejoice that you are privileged to live in this era. Many are unaware of the importance of the times in which they are living. This will all soon change as it will become apparent that something unique and supernatural is about to begin on the face of the earth.

"I am heartened by your response and hope that others will fulfill their calls so that all may be accomplished quickly and for the greater glory of My Father. You will be given many opportunities to fulfill the will of My Father, but do not hesitate in your call. The salvation of many souls is at stake. This is why so many extraordinary graces are being poured forth.

"The era of My Mercy has come. It will unite Heaven and earth in one hymn of love to the Blessed Trinity. I call you to rejoicing. The time has come. So be it. Amen.

"My Mother wishes to speak to you."

Blessed Mother: "My Son's mercy has made it possible for all that is now occurring. The merits of the Saints should be drawn upon by all who are now living so that they can be united in the grand scheme which is unfolding from Heaven.

"Be not afraid to come forward when called. It is by God's mercy and my intercession that many will be saved.

"There will be many attempts to crush this work which is being accomplished through you. Be aware that this will occur. However, it will only aid in the merit of what is being undertaken and will in the end add to its strength as *a movement of love and faith.*

"Remember, in the end only three things will last: faith, hope and love and the greatest of these is love. Love well and you have nothing to fear. Do all out of love so that all your intentions and actions will be in accord with the direct will of God. Love well and have faith that Heaven may accomplish its plan on the face of the earth to the greater glory of God for all eternity. Now go in peace as We bless you."

65

Thursday, June 11, 1987
3:00-3:40 P.M.

"Making Reparation For So Much Sin"

Vision of Our Lord and Our Blessed Mother with Their Sacred and Immaculate Hearts exposed:

Jesus: "Making atonement for sin is not always easy. Reparation must be made to both the Sacred and Immaculate Hearts, if God's justice is to be appeased. I call upon all My faithful followers to help in this awesome task of making reparation for so much sin. Offer your sufferings in addition to your daily duty.

"See the bruises on My face. See what sin has done to Me. How it has caused so much grief to Me and My Most Holy Mother! Repair for this. Heal My wounds inflicted by the soldiers who acted on behalf of all sinners for all time. They tortured Me in a most dreadful fashion, much worse than is now commonly understood. My Mother endured intense pain seeing Me treated in such heinous fashion. I Who was so meek, yet treated so cruelly. Your Creator was made subject to His creatures in order that you might be saved. Such great mercy you cannot fathom.

"Be prepared to suffer as I did. Take up your cross and follow Me. He who would have eternal life must suffer for it. It can be attained in no other way except for the innocent little souls who die in innocency before the age of reason. Take up your cross and follow Me. This is the way it must be. Amen. Now go in peace."

Mariamante: "Lord, please strengthen me to carry the cross in whatever way You wish."

Jesus: "I will. Remember, My yoke is gentle and My burden is light. If you are united to Me, it will become your joy.

"My Mother wishes to speak to you."

Blessed Mother: "My Son gives crosses only to those whom He knows can carry them. See the mercy of your God—that He allows that you may suffer in the redemption of souls while making it your joy. You will understand this better soon and it may not be in the way in which you expect it, but I say to you, there will be rejoicing in Heaven among the Angels and Saints for those who willingly aid in the redemption of souls. Their reward will be great in Heaven and their joy will have no end. I your Mother have said it and I promise this to you this day that you will be counted among the privileged who suffer as my Son, Your Creator, did.

"Peace be with you. Go in peace and do what you are supposed to do."

66

Saturday, June 13, 1987
Feast of St. Anthony of Padua and
Second Apparition of Our Lady of Fatima

"Offer Up The Suffering"

Vision of Our Blessed Mother while on a pilgrimage at a St. Anthony of Padua Church, on his Feast day:

Blessed Mother: "Do not be disquieted by what is going on around you. The tumult is caused by the evil one to try and suppress the work which is about to begin. You must rise above it in order to fulfill my plan. Do not let Father's resistance deter you from your persistence in continuing to fulfill the will of the Lord. I will deal with him directly as he is not open to suggestion from you. Use this time as a means for your own purification and offer up the suffering, that the Apostolate might begin...

"Go now and have no fears, as your little one needs you. But persevere in all that We have instructed you. Go in peace."

67

Thursday, June 18, 1987
12:30-1:00 P.M.

"Purity Of Intentions"

Vision of the Christ Child, then the Blessed Mother:

Christ Child: "I wish to expound on the virtue of charity this day and the need for purity of intentions and all actions of the will. This form of purity has, of course, nothing to do with the physical properties of the flesh, but is of itself in the spiritual realm, as it pertains only to the spiritual side of the nature of man.

"I wish for all My children to have a truly spiritual side of their nature manifested in all their actions. This will be accomplished through the purity of intent of which I now speak. How is this gained, you may ask Me? This is again, as always, gained through prayer.

"Request of Me all that is good for thee spiritually and it will be granted to thee. By My very nature, I am nearly unable to refuse such requests unless they be hampered by the blockage of sin in the individual's soul. In which case, they need only to repent of their sin in the confessional with firm resolve not to sin again in the same fashion, and ask again for the same, that is, the purity of intention which will make all their actions and thoughts in accord with the will of My Father in Heaven.

"My Mother was preserved from the need to even request this, as she wished only to do the will of God in all things from the moment of her Immaculate Conception. However, all others must request this favor from Myself in order to grow closer to God by seeking to fulfill only His will for His glory, rather than for human interest or gain on the part of the individual soul. Once this is established within the individual soul, then the soul may take its flight to Me on the wings of love, as you say in quoting one of My great Saints. She understood this well and made great progress very rapidly due to this facet of her understanding.

"Remember that all you see manifested in My Saints comes direct from Me in regard to their great holiness and virtues. These abilities and capacities are granted by God alone and cannot be gained by the individual without much prayer and sufferings.

"In the worldly sense these sufferings seem frightening to the individual. However, you are beginning to see the beauty in them yourself and can understand that all that is given by God is truly beautiful and given only for the purpose of bringing that soul closer to Me. It is, of course, the individual's response to such trials which account for the gain, stagnation, or loss in the spiritual ascent.

"There is a need today for a clarification of these basic truths, for many are not truly aware of these aspects of the spiritual life. Do not be afraid to speak of spiritual truths and most certainly do read that which has already been written by My Saints, in particular. Their writings were guided by My Holy Spirit; this allowed them to establish great truths in a clear and succinct manner, which all who seriously pursue the spiritual path will be able to understand. I make all that is necessary for you to know to come to Me very easily understood, so that all My children may avail themselves of these gifts I have given to the world, that is, the documentations of the basic truths by My Saints which are great gifts in and of themselves for all My children.

"Be aware of the enemy's intent to stop you and what you are being called to do for Me. He is as a hungry lion looking for someone to devour. Do not give him a chance to work on you as the Scriptures say, and keep your own intentions pure and untarnished by thought of any self gain.

"Desire only the will of God in all things and you will continue to receive direct protection from Myself and My Most Holy Mother. Never allow resentments to hamper your thinking, or you may be taken in by the evil one in most subtle ways."

Mariamante: "Lord, how do I guard against this happening to me?"

Christ Child: "By frequent Confession to keep your soul free and spotless of these imperfections in nature and sins which can grow out of them.

"My Mother wishes to speak to you."

Blessed Mother: "My child, charity will free you from all the evils that would harm you. Practice charity in all things. Love your neighbor as yourself and you will be able to triumph over all the snares the evil one will lay for you. He is most confounded by charity as it is contrary to his nature and understanding, and you will snatch away all victories from his hands by it.

"Practice charity well. Love and holy obedience will continually protect all my children. Amen.

"Now go in peace as We bless you."

68

Monday, June 22, 1987
4:20 P.M.

"Return Love For Love"

Vision of Our Lord with His Sacred Heart exposed:

Jesus: "I wish to hear adoration and praise from the lips of My children. This is heard all too seldom by Me, as many spend much of their time in prayer of petition asking for favors. Yes, it is true I desire to help all My little ones, but have you no time for your Creator alone? Must you be always thinking of others while speaking to Me? I yearn to hear the sweet and kind words of My children and My beloved ones. Would you neglect Me so?

"See the wound in My Heart. How it bled for thee! For each one of thee individually I endured the Cross, yet so many think of Me only when in need of help. I ask of you only one thing, that is, return love for love. Return the love I have given to you in abundance so the full circle of love might be complete, even as it is with the Father and I in Heaven by the union of the Holy Spirit, the love perpetually generated by both of Us creating the union of love. This bond is infinite, never-ending, never-beginning, yet always fresh and new.

"So should your love be for Me in the Holy Trinity. Return the love in spirit and truth which I have given to thee and it shall be the uniting force of thee to the Trinity. I solidify this union of thee to the Trinity by My having become man, taking on your very nature in order to have created the indissoluble bond which will endure for eternity between God and mankind.

"There is so much that you do not know, so much that you need not know. Only that you love Me is all I ask. This is sufficient for the salvation of all mankind, that is, that they love Me above all else in their lives as is rightfully so.

"My Mother has done so much for you. Love her also in return. Tell her that you love her often as it is fitting to love a Mother so.

"Be kind to one another, and do all out of love and you will be made pleasing in My sight.

"My children spend so much time with one another, yet so little time with Me. I wish for this to change. For you will not find the answers in one another, only in Me. You must come to the source of all knowledge and goodness in order to spread true love and devotion throughout the world.

"I ask that you visit Me in the Most Blessed Sacrament each day for a time and spend this time alone in adoration and praise of Me in this Most Holy Sacrament of love. This will bring you ever closer to Me and allow Me to give to you the love I wish to share with all My children.

"I am heartened and pleased to see My children approach Me in this sacrament of love. I wish all to do this for love of Me and in reparation for sin. Come to Me now in this sacrament of love. Let him who has ears hear! Come to Me without hesitation. Come! Amen.

"Now go in peace even as I bless you."

Mariamante: "Lord, I love Thee in the Most Blessed Sacrament."

Jesus: "I know. Continue in this devotion."

Wednesday, June 24, 1987
3:00-3:25 P.M.

69

"The Pope I Love So Dearly"

Vision of Our Blessed Mother:

Blessed Mother: "The barrage of illnesses by which you have been affected and your family, in part, is for your own purification. There is about to be fulfilled one of the prophecies of which I spoke earlier. This will be in regard to yourself. You need not be frightened of what is about to happen to you as it will be from God and will aid in the salvation of the souls of others in addition to your own. Be not afraid. Trust in me and my Divine Son Who loves you so. He is pleased with your response to the trials He has given you and wishes you to now be rewarded for your unswerving loyalty to Him and His Church.

"I have petitioned for your cause on behalf of all mothers and wish now for a greater impetus to be given to my work. You will be surprised and pleased to see the rapidity by which things will begin to move and exhilarated by the response by which it will be received.

"We commend your steadfastness during this difficult period of trial which has now past. Be ready and open to the working of the Holy Spirit at all times now and do not be fearful, so that all may be accomplished without hindrance of human resistance or interference with the work of the Lord. He will not allow anything to happen to you which is not of Him in regards to this particular situation.

"You have been given many indications in the past of that which is about to occur. But you will still be surprised when it occurs. I have prepared your soul as an advocate for many and wish to endow you with extraordinary graces so that all may be accomplished through the children whom I love in a most tender way.

"They will be called forth in great numbers now because the moment has come for my Triumph to gain added momentum, partly due to the extraordinary cooperation and holiness of this Holy Father who is leading so many of my children back to me and my Divine Son. He is the crowning glory of my movement, the Pope I love so dearly, and the one to whom you must refer for all guidance in matters of faith and morals. Give him your unswerving loyalty as my Son's true representative on earth which he is. He will never lead you astray in any way and will never cease to bring all my children closer to me and to their divine reward in eternity.

"Be steadfast in all We have instructed you so far. And be not afraid. Trust and love and you will be rewarded by me in the most personal of ways. Go now in peace and tend to your duties with joy and love."

Mariamante: "I love you, Mother. And please tell Our Lord I love Him."

Blessed Mother: "I will. Go now, my child."

70 *Sunday, June 28, 1987*
3:45-4:20 P.M.

"Pray In Reparation To My Immaculate Heart"

Visions of Our Blessed Mother with Her Immaculate Heart exposed, then dressed as Mother of Sorrows; and Our Lord (although only the Blessed Mother spoke):

Blessed Mother: "There is wisdom in what your Father is telling you. You must listen to him even if at times it may seem difficult. He has been given charge over your soul. This is by divine providence. I want you to do all that he tells you religiously."

I then said the prayer Father told me to say when the visions begin as I had forgotten to do so at the beginning of these. Having heard what the Blessed Mother just said reminded me of this.

Blessed Mother: "You are correct to do this. It is wise to test the spirits, but I am of God and have come only to help you.

"Do not hesitate in fulfilling what We have asked of you. Time is of the essence.

"The other man's role is of confirmation. He will be helpful to you in establishing this Apostolate, for he is being fashioned after my Divine Son. I am not concerned with short delays, only lengthy ones. There is still much time.

"I want all my children to behave as such towards each other, not acting as quarrelling siblings, which is so often the case even in my various apostolates which have been established throughout the world. This only allows room for the evil one to gain a hold and lessen the effectiveness of my work among my children. Do not let him in.

"It is correct that you must be honest with one another, but in a kind way.

"But do not fear, the Apostolate will begin and it will be all that you expected and more. This is because it is of me, and my work is in the name of the Lord Who made Heaven and earth.

"I am saddened now. *My Heart is burdened with so much sorrow* that my children suffer so from so much strife caused by sin. You can all, *members of my Apostolate, lessen this by your prayers. Pray in reparation to my Immaculate Heart for sin in the world, especially those sins against purity and blasphemies against my Divine and adorable Son.*[32]

"How He has suffered for you. You must be grateful for this. Be ever grateful for what God has done for you in sending His only begotten Son to die that you might be set free from your sins. This I can never stress enough. Be grateful. Be kind. Be holy. Do not quarrel.

"Now go in peace, even as I bless you."

Mariamante: "Mama, I love you."

Blessed Mother: "And I love you."

71

Monday, June 29, 1987
11:10 A.M.

"Be Patient"

Vision of Our Lord with His Sacred Heart exposed:

Jesus: "Be patient. In the end, patience will win out."

32. During this message the Blessed Mother begins to address the "members of my Apostolate" directly. Although the information given since these visions began in February is meant for them, it seems notable that she now begins to address them directly. This is, of course, the Apostolate of Holy Motherhood in Catholic Families, which is to be a spiritual movement of mothers, and which was formally announced by the Christ Child during the vision on the Feast of the Annunciation, March 25, 1987, in which He included specific instructions.—Mariamante.

72

Wednesday, July 1, 1987
12:10 P.M.

"Think Only Of Me During Your Prayers"

Vision of Our Lord with His Sacred Heart exposed:

Jesus: "I wish for you to come to Me in all your necessities. Continue to try and think only of Me during your prayers, blocking out all distractions of your daily life. I know your many concerns and have them in My Heart when you pray. You need not differentiate each one of them. Spend your time in adoration, praise, and love of Me, and all else will be taken care of. This includes your temporal needs as well.

"Although the words I speak to you may at times seem contradictory, if you look closely, this is not the case. With the eyes of faith all will be understood."

73

Thursday, July 2, 1987
4:50-5:30 P.M.

"The World Now Needs Respect For Motherhood And Children"

Vision of Our Lord and Our Blessed Mother with Their Sacred and Immaculate Hearts exposed:

Jesus: "I will remove all influence from your life which is not of Me if you allow Me to do so. This requires complete trust in Me that all that happens to you is from Me and allowed for the purpose of bringing you closer to Me. I will continue to work behind the scene, as it were, in order to accomplish this effect in your life. Trust in Me and love Me above all else, and you will have the peace which I wish for you to have at all times, so that My grace can sustain you in all circumstances.

"My Mother's protection of you is constant and never-ending; of this you need not fear, as long as you remain faithful to Me in your call and free from grave sin. I will not allow any harm to come to you, as you are a chosen instrument of My Mother's work. She is fashioning you after Me and My Divine Heart, so that you will be able to carry out what she has planned for you and continues to instruct you to do.

"The resistance of others will also be there to some degree. However, this should not affect you in your zealousness.

"Pray that your Father be open to the working of the Holy Spirit in all facets of his own life, so that he will be able to answer the call which We have given him. He hesitates, which is understandable to some degree, but the time for hesitation to end is near and We will require his work and time in order to accomplish what Heaven has planned. We have demonstrated Our hand in his own life in regards to this work by his recent transfer, thus allowing him more time to tend to this task which must now begin to take precedence in his life.

"Tell him this will aid in the salvation of many souls, as We have said before, much more than he is now able to touch of his own volition in his own life. This is because of the divine inspiration and origin of this work which will allow it to be much more effective than any one person could accomplish in his or her own life.

"Again, I tell you: be thankful that God has chosen you as such instruments. This is a great privilege not to be passed by. . .

"Continue to do all that We have instructed you. My Mother wishes to speak to you."

Blessed Mother: "We will give you several opportunities to fulfill the will of God before His grace is withdrawn in regard to the particular task at hand, no matter what it may be at the time. You are concerned that he has not followed through with what We have asked of him. I will continue to give him the opportunity to remedy this many times before putting another priest in your path who will be willing to follow Our call. This I do not wish to do, as he is Our first choice and has been your spiritual director for some time now. It is only right that he should benefit from the labors he has sustained on behalf of your soul. But Heaven cannot wait forever and these are indeed urgent times as I have said before.

"I too will join you in your prayer that he answer Our call in regard to this work of the Lord. Repeat after Me: I am the handmaid of the Lord. I wish only to do the will of God, and I pray the same for others, especially those closest to me in my life. Amen.

"You may ask Father one more time to consecrate the fraternity to my Immaculate Heart. If he does not respond, do not bring it up again.

"The Apostolate of which We have instructed you is far more important and will involve many more souls than you both can now imagine. Be attentive to this first and work towards fulfilling all that We have instructed you in these visions. By doing so, you will affect the lives of millions of souls throughout the world.

"The world now needs respect for motherhood and children. This will help to offset the tremendous evil which has destroyed so many families. The Apostolate of Holy Motherhood in Catholic Families will bloom like a rose in Heaven.

"Be attentive to Our plans and wishes as We reveal them to you so that all may be accomplished for the greater glory of the Most Holy Trinity in time and in eternity.

"Go now. And remember that We love you and understand your pains. You will be rewarded for your steadfastness as promised."

Mariamante: "Mother, please bless me."

Blessed Mother: "I shall. Now go in peace, my child."

74

Sunday, July 5, 1987
8:50-9:15 P.M.

"Keep Your Eyes Only On My Son"

Vision of Our Blessed Mother with Her Immaculate Heart exposed:

Blessed Mother: "Do not be concerned with what is happening to others. Their relationship with God may be in a different stage than your own and comparison could cause confusion. If you keep your eyes only on My Son you will be drawn closer to Him more rapidly than if you have your eyes on others. Although filial concern is a Christian necessity, it should entail being only concerned with that which will help your brothers and sisters to love God more and never anything else.

"The vanities of this world are many and they can ensnare even the most unlikely if all are not careful. It would be easy for some to become proud or boastful by comparing themselves with others who are perhaps weaker in faith. This is why the importance of silence in regard to spiritual happenings is so great. It allows God to work in the soul in secret, known only to the spiritual director, and then even he will not understand all that is occurring, for who can know the mind of God or fully understand His workings in the human soul.

"I urge you to pray always. Make your life a prayer, a hymn of love for God and to God that He may be glorified in all you do. *Offer Him your every moment of the day in love and reparation and atonement for the sins of the world.* I assure you He will repay you a hundredfold, as you have tasted the generosity of your God. He loves to repay His faithful souls even with surprise gifts of love to adorn their souls for the greater glory of the Most Holy Trinity.

"Our Lord and Saviour Jesus Christ, my Divine Son, must be your example in all things. Look to Him in the reading of Holy Scriptures, meditating upon His holy words. All that was uttered from His sacred mouth must be food for your soul. His words are as balm for the soul, and the dew upon the grass.

"Love Him with your whole heart. Hold nothing back in returning what He has given to you. Be ever grateful for all that He has done for you in fashioning you after Himself. Indeed, this is the case for all His children whom He wishes to solidly establish as members in His Father's kingdom.

"Allow yourself to be molded by His divine hands. Allow the working of the Holy Spirit in your hearts and souls that the transformation may be completed as God wills it so, so that you may be living images of my Divine Son working for the greater glory of God now upon the face of the earth.

"Be joyful in the Lord for He loves you so. Be grateful as He has blessed you so. Be thankful that He has called you all to be members of my holy Apostolate. And remember His words: It is not you that have chosen Me, it is I Who have chosen you.

"Go now in peace to love and serve the Lord. Be at peace that your prayers will be answered, for the Lord is attentive to your pleadings on the behalf of others. Go now in peace."

75

Wednesday, July 8, 1987
3:40 P.M.

"Tend To Your Duties With Love And In Patience"

Vision of Our Lord with His Sacred Heart exposed, followed by Our Blessed Mother:

Jesus: "There is much that you do not know and much that you need not know. That is all right. My Mother and I will reveal to you what is necessary when the time comes for you to know and carry out Our wishes. We do not expect you to understand all that is occurring here. In fact, it would be impossible for you to grasp fully the scope of that which is occurring.

"We are pleased with your efforts thus far in carrying out that which We have instructed you but wish for you to develop an even greater prayer life. This will be facilitated through an influx of grace which will allow you to be in constant union with Us throughout your day in the manner of a contemplative life of prayer.

"My Mother will be your guide in leading you ever deeper into My Sacred Heart. The wound in My Heart will be the opening by which you enter, thus allowing you to experience My mercy on an ever deepening level. This will allow you to act mercifully in accord with your relationships with others. This is how I wish My children to be: merciful towards each other at all times so that forgiveness will come easily and peace and harmony will reign in their hearts at all times. This is what I wish you to practice towards others—mercy and kindness. By doing so you will be able to bring others to Me and set the proper Christian example.

"I know the difficulties of your life. I know the trials and tribulations which you endure, but these only serve to strengthen the faith of My children and should be viewed in such a light. Having the proper perspective will allow you to undergo all things in a calm and peaceful fashion.

"Do not allow others to influence you if you see error in their ways, even if you may admire them greatly for their holiness. Imitate only My example and My Mother. We will form you as We wish and know best. Do not allow yourself to be molded by succumbing to the pressures of those who do not have the

divine perspective as We do. Seek to please Me alone, p
no heed to human respect in any form, and you will see
clearly than if you are concerned with the desires of others.

"There is no need to hurry; be careful that you do not grow impatient, for patience is truly a virtue which should be practiced at all times. My children in the materially developed areas of the world would do better to practice this virtue more readily.

"Be at peace and trust in Me and I will draw you ever closer to Me.

"My Mother wishes to speak to you."

Blessed Mother: "My Son has instructed you in the virtue of patience. This I wish to be practiced among all members of my Apostolate in a special way and to a great degree. Love is patient, love is kind. Remember this well and put it into practice so that in fulfilling your daily duties you will attain a higher perfection. Do all for the glory of God as you carry out your day and it will take on a greater meaning and depth.

"Go now and tend to your duties with love and in patience."

Mariamante: "My Mother, please make me receptive and willing to do the will of God in all things so that I may be made more pleasing to God."

Blessed Mother: "Your prayers have been answered. Now go in peace."

76

Sunday, July 12, 1987
2:30-3:03 P.M.

"The Sacrament Of Penance"

Vision of Our Lord and Our Blessed Mother with Their Sacred and Immaculate Hearts exposed:

Jesus: "My Sacred Heart will be your safe refuge in times of trial and need. Never be afraid to call upon Me even when you feel you have done something wrong, as this is when you are most in need of My Mercy.

"The wound in My Sacred Heart is the manifestation of My Mercy. It was pierced for love of you and all My children so that all can forever call upon Me in their difficulties and sins. I wish to forgive all sins. I wish for all My children to be free from sin, but know that due to your fallen nature this is not always possible. This is why I have instituted the Sacrament of Penance and Reconciliation in My Church so that you may be always reunited to Me after you have fallen into discord through sin.

"Although venial sins do not separate you entirely from Me, I wish for you to confess them so that you will be free from all sin as much as possible. You will always grow closer to Me through this holy sacrament and receive the graces necessary to strengthen you not to fall again in the same fashion.

"My Mother wishes to speak to you of her Apostolate."

Blessed Mother: "Do not be fearful about Father's leaving. This is necessary and will be good for all of you who are closely associated with him. . . .and continue to tell him of all that occurs to you. This is of the utmost importance. Communicate with him in whatever way you can but do not neglect to tell him of all the extraordinary experiences that occur to you. This is the only way in which he will be able to direct you properly.

"I will be giving him an extraordinary grace to aid in the inception of my movement of which I speak here. This will give him great zeal to carry out this task. But first, he must endure the initial suffering which is characteristic of what is necessary in the spiritual realm. That is, the suffering must precede the glory, so to speak, as this is the way in which my Divine Son has established the order in the divine act of redemption. This pattern is for all time to be until the end of time. Then all things will be as new. But as for now, you must endure sufferings in order to grow spiritually and to be fashioned in the likeness of my Son.

"Rejoice in all your trials and count them as blessings in disguise, for, indeed this is what they are. Be not afraid. I am always with you and my Son continues to give you His divine protection which nothing can penetrate except your own sins.

"Stay free from sin and enjoy the grace of God in your souls, so that you may be made more pleasing to Him as time goes on. Let us rejoice in the Lord for He has set you free from your sins.

"Praise Him always. Give Him thanks. Adore Him with all your hearts. Love the Blessed Sacrament and spend time in adoration daily in His presence. Tell Him that you love Him and are grateful for the sacrifice He has made on your behalf.

"Praise the Holy Trinity! And be kind to one another. I love you all. Now go in peace."

Mariamante: "Mother, please bless me and ask Our Lord to bless me too."

Blessed Mother: "I will."

77

Tuesday, July 14, 1987
5:10 P.M.

"Your Family Enclosed In My Heart"

Vision of Our Blessed Mother with Her Immaculate Heart exposed:

Blessed Mother: "Rest in my Immaculate Heart. I have your family enclosed in my Heart."

78

Same day, Tuesday, July 14, 1987
5:30-6:00 P.M.

"Pray That Families Will Have Great Reverence For New Life"

Vision of the Christ Child in the arms of Our Lady of Mt. Carmel:

Christ Child: "Behold, I am the Way, the Truth, and the Life. I am the living testimony of love. Come to Me all who are weary and I will give you rest.

"My Mother wishes to establish this Apostolate so that many children may be spared needless suffering. They are the victims of society in which its members are intent on pleasing only themselves, regardless of the cost to others, even their own children.

"Pray for children, all children throughout the world. They are suffering as in a holocaust, whereby they are sacrificial victims of the greed and selfishness of others. I want this to cease.

"Pray that families will have great reverence for new life, great reverence for children who are fashioned in My image. They enjoy the highest dignity of innocence. This is what you must strive for yourselves, the innocence of children. Strive to be spotless of sin, innocent as little children and blameless in My sight. I say unto you, if you do not have the faith as little children, you shall not enter into My Father's kingdom.

"Families must strive to live together in peace. They should separate for only the most dire circumstances as in the case of violence. But in most cases, this can be avoided by a peaceful reaction even in the face of great difficulties. Never allow children to be harmed. This would be a case for separation.

"Pray for peace in your homes so that you may not have to endure such trials as do splinter so many of today's families.

"There is a lack of reverence which has permeated deep into the whole of society. This will cause destruction and chaos if it is not averted by holy means before it is too late.

"I adjure those who are enlightened in the love of My Mother, those who love Holy Mother Church, of which she is the prototype to perfection, listen to her warnings, her admonishments for peace. Pray the Rosary, wear the Scapular. Do as she tells you so that you will have the peace in your homes and throughout the world.

"Trust in her motherly protection. She is solicitous of your love for Me so that you will be able to enjoy all that has been promised to those who love Me and do the will of My Father in Heaven.

"Be at peace. Love one another and pray always so that the will of God may be accomplished on the face of the earth.

"Now go in peace as I bless you from My Heart."

79

Thursday, July 16, 1987
Feast of Our Lady of Mt. Carmel 1:25 P.M.

"Mother Of The Redeemer Of All Mankind"

Vision of Our Blessed Mother as Our Lady of Mt. Carmel:

Blessed Mother: "My child, be at peace with all that is occurring around you. This will all pass soon and you will experience a period of bliss. The evil one wishes to suppress this work but this he will not accomplish for my power is infinitely greater as I have told you before.

"Be at peace with your daily duty. It is your means of sanctification and the way in which you will be brought closer to God. The Heart of my Divine Son is solicitous of the love of little souls. They charm Him as little children do their parents. He wants all souls to love Him with child-like confidence, not in pride or boastfulness.

"Today is the *Feast of Our Lady of Mt. Carmel. This is an important feast for members of my Apostolate because it signifies the dignity and exaltation of My soul as Mother of God. Motherhood itself has been exalted the day I was begotten for this divine purpose as Mother of the Redeemer of all mankind.* Be at peace and *venerate me under this title* so that you will become more like me, particularly in the realm of your prayer life and fulfillment of daily duty.

"I am the Queen of Heaven and Earth and wish to pour forth graces upon mankind which God has given to me for the preparation of this new Pentecost. Beckon the Holy Spirit with me that He may live in your hearts and souls and bring Jesus Christ my Divine Son to life within you.

"Follow the impulses of the Holy Spirit as He guides you in holiness and virtue. He and I will form the Lord within you if you welcome Us into your hearts. Pray always that this will occur for the world.

"Be at peace and pray. Now go and tend to your work with a recollected sense. Pray to the Holy Spirit to strengthen and inspire your prayer life and He will answer your prayers. Go now, my child."

80

Friday, July 17, 1987
12:50 P.M.

"Be At Peace And Worship Me In The Blessed Sacrament"

Vision of Our Lord with His Sacred Heart exposed:

Jesus: "Rest in My Sacred Heart...

"The desire to leave one's mark in the world has reaped havoc upon My priesthood. This is rooted in pride and is causing Me great grief. Rather than serving Me in obscurity and love, many of My priests wish for acclaim and notice in the world. They wish for the respect from their peers. This is nonsense. They should seek only Me and My will and not be concerned with the attention of the world. Fame is fleeting and contrary to holiness as the world knows it. Many theologians have been seduced by this error.

"Be at peace and worship Me in the Blessed Sacrament as you have been. Continue in your daily duty with joy and strengthen your prayer life with prayers to My Holy Spirit. This will give you the union which you so desire.

"I too am concerned for. . . . If he continues his preoccupation with other less important things, We will put another priest in your path who will give this matter the attention which it deserves. My Mother grieves for those who do not answer her call. Pray that she not grieve this time."

Mariamante: "Lord, please let me adore Thy Sacred Countenance in my heart continually, in reparation and love for all who reject Thee and Thy love."

Jesus: "Yes. Pray for their enlightenment and the renunciation of the sins they commit. Be at peace. You know that I love you."

81

Sunday, July 19, 1987
2:00 P.M.

"My Sacred Heart Is Your Resting Place"

Vision of Our Lord with His Sacred Heart exposed:

Jesus: "Be at peace, My child. I know that this is a great trial for you, but it is necessary for you to be fully united to Me. There is much work to do and I wish to make use of you as an instrument of My Mother's cause. This will require complete filial trust and undying love for Me.

"My Sacred Heart is your resting place and the dwelling of your refreshment. Cling to Me ever so closely as I call your soul to an espoused union of love. Be at peace and rejoice! Do not fear the heights! They are where I dwell and where you must dwell if you are to remain in constant union with Me. The rocky cliff upon which you have climbed is the way to Me. Do not be frightened or discouraged by the steepness of the climb. Be at peace with your struggle. If you but make the effort, I will reach out My hand and grasp you, drawing you closely to Me where you will find your rest and the joy which surpasses earthly pleasures. How shallow they are in comparison to the joy which My love brings to My espoused souls. Blissful and eternal love is yours for the asking, but first you must desire this above all else in your life and proceed in courage and faith in your ascent to Me.

"My Mother has shown you the way. She has prepared My brides for this union of love, to sing praises to God. Hold fast to Me! Cling to nothing or no one else. Call upon My Mother's protection, but think of Me always as your beloved bridegroom.

"The Bridegroom calls His brides to Him; come and dwell with Me on high. Make My Heart your own abode. Stay with Me in love; never leave Me. Think of Me always and I will dwell within you perpetually. I in thee and you in Me and together We will dwell in the Trinity, as the Father has promised Me. Be at peace, you have come home. Amen."

82

Wednesday, July 22, 1987
Feast of St. Mary Magdalene 2:58 P.M.

"There Is No Sin Which Cannot Be Forgiven"

Vision of Our Lord with His Sacred Heart exposed:

Jesus: "My divine compassion wishes to enfold all sinners. I long for their return home. There is no sin which cannot be forgiven.[33] Witness the example of My beloved St. Mary Magdalene. Her greatest privilege was to be the first to see Me risen from the dead. This honor was reserved for her by the merits of her love and true contrition. Her courage and faith saved her. Often it takes courage for an individual to admit the wrong they have done, especially in the presence of others. This was her case. You are fortunate to be able to confess your sins in private in the confessional without the stares of on-lookers.

"I do not ask for public admission of guilt, only that you come to Me privately in the confessional, speaking to Me in the person of the priest present, and I am eager to absolve you of your sins. This most merciful means of admission of guilt and cleansing of sin is without fault or imperfection. This is divinely instituted by Myself so that sinners would forever have

33. A correct understanding of the "unforgivable sin," the blasphemy against the Holy Spirit, can be found in the following excerpt from Pope John Paul II's Encyclical on the Holy Spirit: "...'blasphemy' does not properly consist in offending against the Holy Spirit in words; it consists rather *in the refusal to accept the salvation which God offers to man through the Holy Spirit,* working through the power of the Cross" *(Dominum et Vivicantem, #46).*—Ed.

the means to come to Me and experience the personal forgiveness which this sacrament offers. This is the only means by which you can be truly assured of My forgiveness. The requirement to express and expel the sins in the confessional individually is the means by which you are known to be forgiven, all sacraments being an outward sign of My grace. Make frequent use of this sacrament and know My love and forgiveness that will bring you the only true peace on the earth.

"Continue in your prayers and pray that sinners make use of this sacrament. Many need to return to My grace in this fashion before receiving Holy Communion. To receive Holy Communion while not in a state of grace is an outrage and a mortal sin. This is occurring on a frequent basis now within My Church and causes Me great distress. Do not allow this to continue. Pray for sinners and their awareness, so that this will cease.

"All members of My Mother's apostolates, pray for sinners and an end to this calamity that has befallen My Church, that is, the reception of Holy Communion by so many who are not in a state of grace. Invoke the Saints in this struggle for justice. This is justice in the spiritual nature and realm. Pray for souls to have true contrition for their sins and to make use of the confessional. My Mercy is boundless. Now go in peace as I bless you from My Heart."

Mariamante: "Lord, I am an unworthy sinner, but I love You and trust in Your mercy. Have mercy on me."

Jesus: "I already have; and I love you. Now go and tend to your work."

83

Friday, July 24, 1987
Feast of St. Christine 1:25 P.M.

"Holy Obedience"

Vision of Our Lord and Our Blessed Mother with Their Sacred and Immaculate Hearts exposed:

Jesus: "The true test of obedience is in conforming one's will to the will of God through the voice of superiors even when the individual may disagree or not understand clearly the meaning of the restriction or chastisement. This strengthens the soul in a unique way by renunciation of one's own will in deference to the will of God as expressed through his or her superiors.

"I am most pleased with this type of self-sacrifice, as it is similar to My own response in the Garden of Gethsemene. Of course, having the divine perspective as I did, I was in complete understanding of the future and the need for My Self-sacrifice. And yet, in My humanity, I knew the pain and suffering to be inflicted upon Me would necessitate the complete subjection to the Divine Will and the acquiescence to My Divine Nature."

At this point there were some interruptions by my children, which brought about the following conversation:

Jesus: "Be at peace with your daily duty. This[34] does not distress Me, why should it you?"

Mariamante: "Lord, because it shocks my soul when I am constantly interrupted."

Jesus: "Be at peace. Do not be angry. This is sometimes a test of the renunciation of your own will in keeping with your daily duty.

"To continue My discourse: This subjection of the will to the ultimate and complete authority of God is best tested in trial and strengthened by the same means. This is often manifested in the lives of My religious and priests, who are most likely to experience this. However, among those who are being drawn closer to Me by My own power, they will often experience this and should be most grateful for the protection which holy obedience affords them in the spiritual realm.

"This protection is by divine institution and is not subject to whether the individual soul is in agreement in all things with the superior or spiritual director or confessor, but is rather a test of conformity of the will of the individual to My will and that of My Father in Heaven.

"I have shown you the way, and you need not fear that I would allow any harm to come to My children whom I am protecting in this fashion. This, of course, refers to matters that are not in contrast to faith or morals. These cases would be few and are not which I refer to here.

"Therefore, be at peace in regards to all matters of holy obedience. I will be the one guiding your pathway and purifying your soul on its way to Me by this means. Rejoice and be thankful that you have such direction and treat your superiors with

---

34. The children's interruptions.—Mariamante.

the respect they deserve as being in My image. Do not discuss their personal faults with others, for who is without fault? This only creates a climate in which arrogance can be fostered. Rather, if you notice a particular defect or weakness, pray for them that they will overcome this and be made more like Me, but never mention it to others. I encourage all My children to be obedient and respectful. This pleases Me very much and causes the Angels to rejoice.

"In regards to your own children, treat them with kindness but be firm or they will direct you instead of you directing them.

"I have given the gifts of spiritual direction to My priests and I wish for them to use them. Never allow a layperson to direct you in spiritual matters. They have no authority to do so. Remain only under the direction of priests. They alone have been given this authority by Me over the laity. In religious houses, such as convents, there is a difference, but you need not be concerned with this here, as this work is for the laity and not fully applicable to religious whom, of course, have superiors within their own order who are not always priests. Yet they too must rely only on confessors—priests—to some degree also and in some matters.

"Be at peace with what is happening to your Father. He will be all right. Continue in prayer and tending to your daily duties and allow Me to work in your life. My Mother will continue to guide and mold you. Listen to her carefully."

Blessed Mother: "This movement will soon begin despite present hardships. I am pleased with Father's response in the heart and will use his sufferings to help others. Disseminate this material quickly, so that others may be helped by the wisdom expressed herein. Do not be fearful or timid. The response you receive will be of my own making. While at first it may begin slowly, the movement will gain momentum with time and will eventually help a great number to love God more and fulfill His will for them.

"I am grateful for the generous souls who respond yes to my call. Come, let us adore Him Who made Heaven and earth, my beloved Son and your Saviour, Our Lord Jesus Christ. Amen."

84

Sunday, July 26, 1987
12:57 P.M.

"Be Totally Abandoned To The Divine And Direct Will Of God"

Vision of Our Lord with His Sacred Heart exposed:

Jesus: "What you have surmised is correct. Some paths will be opened while others will be blocked. This is My own work to keep you and others on the path to Me. Oftentimes a soul does not know what is best for him or her and they will stray from the most direct route to Me. If a soul makes the intention as an act of the will to do only My will, they will be brought along by Me directly; and this is one of the means which I employ.

"You may often be startled at first as to why a particular path which formerly seemed so clear and safe is now being blocked, but you need only to trust in Me that this is My direct will which is allowing it to be so, and allow Me to work in your life. If a soul resists and continues on a path which is being blocked, it serves only to stunt their own spiritual growth. Rather, acceptance is what is needed, and you will soon experience a peace about what is occurring.

"That is not to say that at times one must not struggle somewhat, and even at times with the evil one himself who will try, particularly among My holy souls or chosen ones to prevent them from carrying out My will, but this you can often surmise intellectually. If a particular soul is about to embark on a glorious or specific task chosen by Me, they can at times expect much resistance. This will soon become evident though, and not a great deal of discernment is necessary to unmask the resistance or work of the evil one.

"However, now I speak of the resistance in the individual soul, when he or she is not pleased with the path which God has chosen for them and continues to resist and find themselves losing ground spiritually because of it. This is very dangerous and should be remedied immediately upon the soul's recognition of this occurring. When one finds that oneself has been resisting the will of God Himself, he or she must make a firm purpose of amendment to no longer do so, and they will find a blessed peace in having done so. Then I will again be truly able to bring the soul along closer to Me.

"Therefore, if a particular path is being blocked by means beyond your control or ability to change, after prayer and resolution that allows you to become abandoned to My will, you should be at peace about it and pursue that which is being opened up for you. In this way, certain inordinate affections of the heart are cleansed and new bonds are made which I Myself have chosen for the individual. Remember: a firm resolve to do only My direct will, will bring about this guiding light which is I Myself in your life.

"Employ My Mother's assistance in all matters of discernment and protection and ask the Saints for their assistance also.

"It is not always easily understood when My will seems to bring about a sudden and irrevocable change in one's life, but trust will bring one through and allow the soul to cast itself totally abandoned in My care. This is true bliss to the soul who truly loves Me above all else, and they will recognize this sort of trial as pure gain after little reflection.

"Therefore, be totally abandoned to the divine and direct will of God at all times, and experience the joy of relying totally and only on your Creator Who alone knows what is best for you.

"Be at peace and hope in My love for you. It is yours for the asking to be experienced by all who call upon Me in sincerity and truth. Amen.

"Now go in peace as I bless you from My Heart."

Mariamante: "Lord, please let me be always totally abandoned to Your holy will at all times and in all circumstances."

Jesus: "Your prayer will be answered because you have asked of it in true faith. You must go now."

85

Wednesday, July 29, 1987
2:25-3:05 P.M.

"The Suffering Of Innocent Children Must Be Mitigated Now"

Vision of Our Lord with His Sacred Heart exposed:

Jesus: "The path least often traveled is the swiftest one to Me. This requires complete renunciation of self-will in deference to My own. I wish to draw souls quickly to Me, but encounter much resistance so often. They cling to the things of earth, to creatures or worldly pleasures. They are easily confused and often stray from the path to Me because their desire to do My will wanes in accord with the weakness of their flesh and their enjoyment of earthly pleasures. These pleasures can be oh so ever slight, and with those already further along the spiritual path, often take the disguise of being efficacious for the salvation of souls, or even a guise of devotion to one's duty, when they are, in fact, a distraction from pursuing My direct will.

"Holy souls, beware! That is, particularly those consecrated to My Mother and belonging to her sodalities and movements. The evil one will use devious means by which to ensnare even the most unlikely. He will make you feel overwhelmed with a false guilt for doing even the slightest action, if it be solely for the glory of God for which it is being carried out. He will forever harass the soul with thoughts that one should be carrying out one's daily duty instead of this particular devotion, prayers, or spiritual nourishment. Beware! He is after those with fervor in order to whittle down their devotion to a lukewarm and ordinary level under this guise of devotion to daily duty as being the only means to Me. Whereas, it is often through one's daily duty that your sanctification should be worked out, it is only in accord with the entire framework of the spiritual life and should be at all times subordinate to the spiritual means. That is, lift your daily duty to the heights by joining your every moment with the contemplation of heavenly things, but do not see it[35] as a pure enough means to Me without constant prayer being employed.

"The frequent reception of the sacraments of Reconciliation and Penance and Holy Communion are the surest and safest way to Me, along with constant prayer and abandonment to the Divine Will in all things. This is your daily duty in the spiritual sense.

"Be at peace with what is occurring with Father. His hesitation is unwarranted at this point, but I have granted him a reprieve because of his sincerity. The next two months will be difficult for you in this respect, but if at the end of this time period which he has expressed, he continues in the neglect of this work, We will regretfully place the other priest in your path whom My Mother has chosen. We know this will cause you grief at first, but the work of God must continue despite all adversity.

35. The daily duty alone.—Mariamante.

"Use this time to pray for the inception of this movement and accompanying Apostolate, and keep your will completely aligned with the Divine Will. Pray the same for others, especially your Father and those closest to you.

"The suffering of innocent children must be mitigated now upon the face of the earth or a grave chastisement will take place. This is one of Heaven's plans to prevent this from occurring and to rescue those who are currently suffering so unjustly.

"My Mother has petitioned the Heavenly Father on behalf of the innocent children throughout the world. This work is for their benefit and must continue despite human resistance.

"You may tell this to Father if you wish but silence is the better way. Let him read it himself. Do not as yet speak to your new confessor.[36] For the time being, just watch and pray for the world."

Mariamante: "Lord, please let me do your direct will in all things."

Jesus: "I will breathe into you My Holy Spirit to strengthen you and give you fortitude and wisdom. And remember, maintain silence when at all possible so that I may speak to you in the whispers of the heart. Now go in peace as I bless you from My Heart."

Mariamante: "Lord, may I speak to Mr. _____?"

Jesus: "Not as yet. Now go and pray."

86

Friday, July 31, 1987
12:45-1:30 P.M.

"Look To The Holy Father For Your Guidance"

Vision of the Christ Child and Our Blessed Mother:

Christ Child: "All truth stems from Me. I am the Truth and those who love truth will be drawn to Me. If a soul is sincerely seeking the truth, he will eventually find Me. However, many have lost the desire for this quest and are content to live on a super-

---

36. When Our Lord said, "Do not as yet speak to your new confessor," in reference to the messages, this is in accord with the same directive my spiritual director at that time, had earlier expressed.—Mariamante.

ficial level, whereby all experience comes through the senses of the flesh and the intellect. Thereby they have caused the cessation of their own spiritual journey, seeking only that which is in the physical sphere or understanding on a merely human level. This serves to make them shallow in their beliefs, so that when challenged, they easily succumb to any error or heresy which is presently being set before them. Their rock, instead of being Me and the successors to the Holy See, the Sovereign Pontiff, are their own feelings and experiences rather than the truth which is Mine and has been set forth by the legitimate authorities in My Church, that is, the Holy Father and the Magisterium of the Church.

"Look to the Holy Father for your guidance. He has been chosen for this purpose to shepherd My flock, and must be the one to whom you look for verification of what is the truth. Do not be led astray by those who would have you believe there is no longer any authority in My Church to teach what is right and wrong, correct or incorrect. These are misguided souls who expound these beliefs, that all things must be subject to the individual's own experience in order to be valid. This is nonsense and not worthy of My true followers' belief.

"Believe in Me. Trust in Me. Hope in Me and My Holy Catholic Church, led by the successor to Peter on whom I founded it. He is your guiding light in the present darkness which has grown so great as even to envelope many of My faithful followers of days gone by. They have sadly succumbed to the modernist heresy.

"Beware! All My faithful and good followers, there are wolves in sheep's clothing who will lead many astray if they are not continuously fortified spiritually for the battle of truth to triumph. Seek Me in the sacraments, particularly the Eucharist and holy Confession, where it is that your light will come directly from Myself to the individual soul.

"Pray often for My Church to be revitalized by My Truth through these two sacraments. This is the means by which holiness will return to all My children.

"I can barely tolerate any more. All Heaven is distressed by the darkness and shallowness which follows, that is enveloping the world and has even crept into My Church by neglect of these sacraments. Worship Me in the Blessed Sacrament and go to Confession frequently, at least once a month for the devotions of First Friday and First Saturday, and see the heavens open up with the light of truth for all to see. Be living images of Me in a world darkened by sin. Be the lampstand not hidden but revealed for all to see so as to guide others to Me.

"There is a voice calling in the wilderness to the world to repent and be enlightened to the truth which is Mine. Answer the call today and listen to your conscience. Amen.

"Now go in peace after My Mother speaks to you."

Blessed Mother: "My soul magnifies the Lord and my spirit rejoices in God my Saviour for He has looked with favor upon His lowly servant. Imitate me in this prayer of thanksgiving and joy with being chosen by God to do His work upon earth.

"The laxness of my clergy must cease in the Church in order for the truth to shine as lights in the night. My message to my priest sons is this: live your vocation to the fullest extent of holiness to which God wishes you to attain. Do not be concerned with matters of the world but with matters of the spirit. Seek spiritual solutions to the problems which the laity come to you with. Help them to grow closer to my Son through frequent reception of the sacraments. This is the purest and most direct path, and in many cases the only answer.

"Do not be as secular counselors to your spiritual children, but as guiding lights to love of the most holy sacraments of the Church. In this they will find their answers and the strength of my Son Himself, Who promised help to all who call upon His Name in faith when He said: 'Come to Me all who are weary and find life burdensome and I will give you rest.' Allow the Lord Himself to refresh these souls and fortify them for their journey heavenward. This is the way to Him Whom you are to represent at all times.

"Do not become as members of the laity yourselves under the falsehood of being more accessible and willing to help. Be the nation set apart that was designed to call souls to the higher level of consciousness of the matters of the spirit instead of the world.

"Be at peace, members of my apostolates, both clergy and laity alike, and seek the truth through the means my Beloved Son has entrusted to the Church, the sacraments. Love what is holy and become holy yourselves. Be good.

"Now go in peace as We bless you."

Mariamante: "Mother, what should I do about the carbon copies?"

Blessed Mother: "You may keep copies yourself to ensure that none are lost, but notify your Father of this action. Now go in peace after Our blessing."

87

Sunday, August 2, 1987
2:55 P.M.

"Renunciation Of Earthly Pleasures And Attachments"

Vision of Our Lord with His Sacred Heart exposed:

Jesus: "Do not allow your anger to overcome you and to influence what is occurring here. While there is such a thing as just anger, even this should dissipate in a short amount of time so as not to create a barrier between the individual soul and God. Resentments form extreme barriers to spiritual growth and must be avoided at all costs. The graces in the confessional will accomplish this within the soul and adherence to this practice by the individual will assure its not occurring.

" 'Vengeance is Mine says the Lord.' If there is any recompense to be made, it will be collected by the taskmaster himself rather than another servant. I will call all to account when the time comes and sometimes sooner than one might think.

"I am distressed with the handling of the present situation and will tend to the matter Myself. I have warned so many so often and have even sent My Mother, yet Our pleadings go unheard. Is there no one who wishes to do the will of God on the face of the earth? Even My chosen souls busy themselves with worldly cares and pleasures. Where are those who wish only to love Me? 'Thou canst not serve God and mammon both.' Listen to your Seraphic Father Francis and choose poverty over riches. Do not cling to the things of this earth but only to Me.

"When I speak here I am referring to others and not to yourself so be at peace. I know that you have chosen Me above all else. Oh that I wish others would do the same! They would spare themselves such grief and many sufferings if they would but choose this pure path to Me of renunciation of earthly pleasures and attachments.

"Follow the example of My Saints who lived in austerity and suffered great penance for the love of God. I do not wish you to bring harm to yourselves, but penance are in order whether it be simple abstinence or fast or abstinence from earthly pleasures. These can be the attachments which impede the flight of the soul of the individual to Me and must be done away with. I am concerned for those who have been given much yet resist in doing My will."

88

Monday, August 3, 1987
3:30-4:10 P.M.

"Come To Me In The Power Of My Holy Spirit"

Vision of the Christ Child and Our Lady of Mt. Carmel:

Christ Child: "I have come that all may have life. These words echo through the ages and are as meaningful now as ever. There is but one path to the Father and it is through the Son. Do not let anyone dissuade you in this belief which is a basic tenet of the Catholic faith. My Mother's role as co-redemptrix and mediatrix of all grace in no way lessens but strengthens one's belief in My role as Saviour and King and center of the universe.

"Before all began, I was. I saw all creation come into being by My Father's almighty hand and witnessed the creation of the Angels. The plan for salvation of mankind was in the bosom of the Trinity from the beginning of time due to the foreknowledge of God. Yet, your Redeemer was saddened and hurt in the personal sense by the fall of man with the first sin of Adam and Eve. Just as today I am still saddened and hurt by those offenses committed by so many against God. This plan of love, of both creation and redemption, continues until the end of time unfolding in the fashion deigned by the Eternal Father for the purpose of the salvation of souls—the eternal bliss to be rewarded to all those who persevere to the end.

"While the divine act of redemption has once and for all been accomplished by Myself at the will of the Father, I continue to send the Holy Spirit to guide those now living to their eternal home.

"Come to Me in the power of My Holy Spirit. Pray that the Holy Spirit guide you in all your endeavors, so that the supreme goal of all your actions will be in pleasing God alone. Seek the Divine Assistance which is at your beckoning in the power of the Holy Spirit. The Spirit intercedes, praying for those who call upon My Name. The Holy Spirit makes available to you the ability to pray forcefully and with conviction and faith, so that your prayer and works will be fruitful.

"Call upon Me that I may breathe the Holy Spirit into your hearts and enlighten your minds, purifying your souls to seek only that which is holy.

"My Mother wishes to speak to you."

Blessed Mother: "My Divine Child has revealed His Spirit to His followers of today as of old. Together with the Holy Spirit I now beckon His return in the hearts of all who call upon me for assistance. I will make your journey to the Father more pleasing in His sight, by the union of my own prayers and supplications, both to and through my Divine Son. He calls upon me to do this. He wishes for me to intercede for you that you may be made more pleasing in His sight. Open your hearts to the Holy Spirit through my intercession. Call upon the Holy Names of Jesus and Mary to be imprinted forever in your hearts by the power of the Holy Spirit. Seek that which is holy above all else. Now go in peace as We bless you."

Mariamante: "My Mother, grant that I may ever love thee and Our Lord more and more."

Blessed Mother: "I will continue to intercede for you, my child. Now go in peace."

89

Saturday
August 8, 1987

"Do Not Resist The Will Of God"

Vision of the Christ Child:

Christ Child: "My most tender child, do you want this movement to begin? Do you want this work to begin for the betterment of the spiritual lives of countless souls? Then you must give up all earthly attachments, including those to all individuals who are not acting in accord with My will in this regard. We told you this would at first cause you great grief and so it will, but it is necessary to go forward with choosing those who will be willing to serve My Mother's cause and be of assistance to her work rather than resistance to the will of God. This is an unfortunate circumstance but one which sometimes occurs, and which is out of your hands in that it involves the will of others. But the work of the Lord which My Mother has conceived in her Heart must go on despite earthly resistance, and sometimes this entails changing persons to be involved.

"You have done the right thing in having the novena of Masses said, but at this point it will only serve to keep him in the picture, but not as one who will be the sole instrument in the preparation of materials for the movement as had been previously planned.''

Mariamante: ''Lord, this seems so cold. Can it not be changed?''

Christ Child: ''We will see what transpires in the next few days, but it is now necessary to bring another priest into the picture as the situation now stands. Be sure that you yourself do not resist the will of God, and continue to pray for the world and the inception of this movement and all those to be involved with bringing it to fruition through My Mother's intercession.

''Go now and tend to your duties. Your child has awakened.''

90

Monday, August 10, 1987
2:50-3:20 P.M.

''Women Of Prayer For The World And The Salvation Of Souls''

Vision of Our Lord and Our Blessed Mother with Their Sacred and Immaculate Hearts exposed:

Jesus: ''I call all My children to come to Me now, seeking safe refuge in the abyss of love which is My Sacred Heart. The forces of evil unleashed upon the world today due to the tremendous amount of sin, is too much for you to combat alone. You must seek safe haven within My Most Sacred Heart and My Mother's Immaculate Heart. Here you will find your protection and freedom from the enslavement which is sin in all its manifestations in the world today.

''Do not be persuaded by those less loyal to Me and to the precepts and teachings of My Holy Church, but be stouthearted and resilient in the midst of this great battle which is now being waged upon the face of the earth for the salvation of millions of souls. Your eternity is at stake. Pay heed to what I and My Mother are telling you so that you will not be caught unawares.

''The wickedness which is so rampant will soon be crushed as My Mother and her cohorts, the Holy Angels, continue to crush the head of the serpent; yet there are many who will perish if they are unaware of the gifts of grace available through the sacraments of My Church for the purpose of making souls holy and able to withstand the terrible assaults of the enemy.

"If you wish to be holy, choose your companions wisely. Do not be taken in or have your faith whittled down by bad company. A person's friend should be like him.

"I do not wish for My housewives to evangelize in the world. This is not their call. They should evangelize with prayer from the heart in their homes, where they are protected from the unnecesary evils and stresses of the world that I do not wish them to come in contact with. Those called to the active apostolate of evangelization are, for the most part, priests. This is not the call for those called to be members of this My Mother's Apostolate of Holy Motherhood. Do not be persuaded by those who would have you think otherwise and offer arguments to the contrary. You have been chosen for the vocation in which you are presently, that is, mothers and housewives, to be women of prayer for the world and the salvation of souls.

"Pray that the iniquity in the world end so that there will be peace upon the face of the earth. There cannot be peace with the great amount of sin which is now being committed throughout the world. Heed My Mother's warnings at Fatima and elsewhere. Prayer and penance, especially the Rosary, and frequent reception of the sacraments is your answer to perfection of daily duty, which you are called to now by My Mother.

"Be at peace. My Mother wishes to speak to you."

Blessed Mother: "My child, there is so much work that needs to be done. Are you willing to participate in this salvific action by your own sufferings and crosses which God chooses to send you?"

Mariamante: "Yes Mother; but please strengthen me to carry the cross as Our Lord wishes, without complaint."

Blessed Mother: "Then I shall give you the peaceful resignation which is necessary to suffering without complaint."

Mariamante: "Mother, please grant me the graces necessary to do all that Our Lord wishes for me to do."

Blessed Mother: "Then I will continue to be your advocate and you will have much to bear, but you will triumph in the end by the power of God which is love. Love those who persecute you and you will know a secret to happiness and the true joy which comes from God alone. My Son knows of all your trials so be at peace with them. Now go in peace as We bless you from Our Hearts."

Mariamante: "Mama, don't leave! I'm frightened."

Blessed Mother: "There is no need to be frightened, for the power of God will be with you. Choose your friends wisely and pray, and do not take anyone into your confidence whom you cannot trust completely. I will remain your Protectress in all circumstances. Now go in peace without fear, but in confidence to love and serve the Lord Our God."

91

Tuesday, August 11, 1987
Feast of St. Clare of Assisi 8:00-8:25 P.M.

"My Triumph Is At Hand"

Vision of the Christ Child and Our Lady of Mt. Carmel:

Blessed Mother: "Peace be with you. Behold the Child Jesus, this Child of love, visible image of the Heavenly Father. He will be your guide to the Father by His example of love manifested so perfectly in His earthly existence.

"Be attentive to the Holy Spirit in your lives so that you will be able to accomplish what He expects of you. You should be eager to do the will of God in all things. Pray that you have this willing spirit, and strengthen the flesh with fast and abstinence from those foods not necessary in your daily diet.

"Be at peace with what is happening this weekend. This great feast has been chosen as a special day for me and a great number of graces will be granted to those now living on the earth. My Triumph is at hand.

"This Feast of the Assumption will be a great feast indeed for it will facilitate a great outpouring of grace to those my faithful followers and children of my Son. Rejoice for these are great and wondrous times in which you are living, as my Triumph is at hand, gaining momentum daily with each soul who answers yes to my call. Comply with the Holy Angels in this struggle against evil and all manner of wickedness. Be alert and do not be deceived by him who opposes my holy forces, the Holy Angels.

"Call upon St. Michael to deliver you from the evil one.

"My Son wishes to speak to you."

Christ Child: "My most Holy Mother is a cause for joy to all the Heavenly Angels and Blessed Spirits. They wait upon her word to do her will which is at all times the will of God. They are her legions of Blessed Spirits called upon to wage this battle for your souls. Be attentive to the working of the Holy Angels in your lives. They will help you to accomplish what God has planned for you in your life.

"Enter the light which is grace on the true and perfect path to the Father. Sing with one accord the hymn to the Father that is your life to be offered up to God for others with love for all to see. Rejoice on this My Mother's Feast of the Assumption. She has much in store for you. Continue to follow her decrees and instructions. She will lead you to Me in eternity.

"Call upon the Saints in your present struggle. They and the Holy Angels will assist you.

"Now go in peace as We bless you from Our Hearts."

CONSECRATION TO THE MOTHER OF GOD

O Exalted Mother of God, Queen of Heaven and Earth, Mother of Our Lord Jesus Christ, I consecrate myself to thee this day and humbly ask thee to take me under thy constant care and protection as thy devoted child.

O tender Mother of Our Redeemer, fill me with thy love for your beloved Son and make me into a likeness of Him and thyself. Fashion my heart after thy Heart. Make it tender, pure, gentle, and kind. Give me great reverence for life, and devotion to duty.

O Spouse of the Holy Spirit, fill me with thy virtues that by the power of the Holy Spirit I may become a true spouse of Jesus Christ.

O Star of the Sea, guiding light, ever guide me into a deeper union with Jesus that I may glorify Him in time and eternity for the greater glory of the Most Holy Trinity, now and forever. Amen.

St. Joseph, pray for us.
All ye Holy Angels and Saints, pray for us.

OTHER SUITABLE PRAYERS FOR THE MOVEMENT

by Mariamante

O Holy Christ Child, enlighten our minds and hearts to the great dignity of children, who are cast in Your image. Let us love and guide them as we ought for Your greater glory.

O Holy Spirit, Spouse of the Mother of God and our Mother, inflame our hearts with Your Divine Love and make us into images of Jesus Christ.

Heavenly Father, make us ever faithful to Your Divine Will and give us great zeal with which to carry it out.

Dearest Lord Jesus, keep us always faithful to all the teachings of Your Church that we may live the life You wish for us now and in eternity. Amen.

Come Lord Jesus. Come and dwell within our hearts.

THE RIEHLE FOUNDATION...

The Riehle Foundation is a non-profit, tax-exempt, charitable organization that exists to produce and/or distribute Catholic material to anyone, anywhere.

The Foundation is dedicated to the Mother of God and her role in the salvation of mankind. We believe that this role has not diminished in our time, but, on the contrary has become all the more apparent in this the era of Mary as recognized by Pope John Paul II, whom we strongly support.

During the past four years the foundation has distributed books, films, rosaries, bibles, etc. to individuals, parishes, and organizations all over the world. Additionally, the foundation sends materials to missions and parishes in a dozen foreign countries.

Donations forwarded to The Riehle Foundation for the materials distributed provide our sole support. We appreciate your assistance, and request your prayers.

IN THE SERVICE OF JESUS AND MARY
All for the honor and glory of God!

The Riehle Foundation
P.O. Box 7
Milford, OH 45150